ENDORSEMENTS

When I began reading "The Invitation" in Antonio Baldovinos' book, *Relentless Pursuit,* my heart burned with hunger to know Christ more intimately, just as the subtitle suggested: *Awakening Hearts to Burn for Him.* I desire my heart to burn more and more for Him. If that is your desire too, I highly recommend this book.

PATRICIA KING
Founder, XPministries

This is a great book! It will provoke desire for God and cause you to search for Him. Most importantly, however, you will understand that more than anything, He desires you. And people who understand this reality are unstoppable. This book unveils the power that will unlock the greatest missions movement of our generation.

STACEY CAMPBELL
Author of *Praying the Bible: The Book of Prayers* and *Praying the Bible: The Pathway to Spirituality*

Antonio's inspiring book *Relentless Pursuit* is a prophetic invitation to go against the stream of watered-down Western Christianity and journey into the depths of the heart of God. May a generation answer the call of these pages and launch into the depths of love for Jesus!

RICK PINO
Fire Rain Ministries

Relentless Pursuit is a clear word from heaven to this generation. In First John 4:19, John clearly lays out that *"we love Him, because He first loved us."* The secret to radically pursuing God is first receiving His radical pursuit of us. Antonio takes us on a journey through this book of how God can take a cold heart, caught up in the religious machine and see it set on fire with His love. I also love how we are given tools in this book to sustain and enflame the pursuit of God in our lives. Antonio actually gives us ways to go after God in a consistent way. I believe that many will look back at this book in the coming decades as one of those words that shifted their relationship with God. I highly recommend this book and this author to you, and pray that God would awaken God's relentless pursuit all over the earth!

COREY RUSSELL
Senior Leadership Team at
International House of Prayer Kansas City

Antonio is one of our cutting-edge leaders in the realm of reaching and discipling youth in this generation. His book will inspire you, inform you, and challenge you to move in with God's movement.

LOREN CUNNINGHAM
Founder, Youth With A Mission (YWAM)

Not often does a man with as much global spiritual experience in world missions and evangelism as this one write such a searching book about the fundamental missing of our heart. Antonio Baldovinos' *Relentless Pursuit* is a kind of 21st-century *Pilgrim's Progress* for one who has not just begun this Christian journey, but walked the road and fought the fight true and long. We want to do more than *begin* well; we want to *end* well also. We seek in such a call not revival; but the One who begins it.

WINKIE PRATNEY
Ministry of Helps

If there is one book that I can say captures the heart of what the Holy Spirit is saying to the Church at large today, it is Antonio

Baldovinos' *Relentless Pursuit.* His passion for intimacy is contagious! This book is destined to become one of the major voices for the next move of God.

CINDY JACOBS
Generals International

Regardless of whether you are already pursuing or have a desire to start pursuing the Almighty, *Relentless Pursuit* is your catalyst! It challenges you to dig deep and not go with the status quo, and in the end you will find fulfilling joy in the fact the Almighty pursues you!

JEREMY AFFELDT
Pitcher, San Francisco Giants, Major League Baseball;
Two-time World Series Champion;
and Founder of Generations Alive

We are about to embark on a glorious new wave of Holy Spirit power and Antonio Baldovinos' book, *Relentless Pursuit* provides the motivation, anticipation, and knowledge to be prepared to experience everything God has planned "for such a time as this." Bob and I are thankful for Antonio's diligence, passion, and boldness to embrace the richness of God's invitation that is available to each one of us! We highly endorse this book to ready hearts for the manifest presence of God on this earth.

AUDREY AND BOB MEISNER
TV hosts, *My New Day*; Best-selling authors,
Marriage Under Cover

Seldom in my many years and ministry experiences on this planet have I read a book from a young man so full of wisdom, passion, and understanding of what it means to know Him. I am reminded of the apostle Paul's journey as I read *Relentless Pursuit: Awakening Hearts to Burn for Him.* Not that their lives were similar, nor the circumstances, but the passion for Truth is. Antonio is challenging us to pursue the heart and faith of Christ. Nothing is more important in the day in which we live. By utilizing the stories of the greats in the history of the Church who have the same inclination and desire, my brother sharing his own life story, Antonio has made this book come alive. I could hardly put it down. I trust every reader will be challenged to seek Christ with all their heart, and then to serve Him with all their might.

TOM PHILLIPS
Vice President, Billy Graham Library

"It's the glory of God to conceal a matter, but the glory of kings to search it out..." Antonio invites us into the glorious treasure hunt that is Christianity—a stunning invitation into a life of hunger for God.

CORY ASBURY
Worship Pastor, New Life Church

RELENTLESS PURSUIT

RELENTLESS PURSUIT

Awakening Hearts *to* Burn *for* HIM

Antonio Baldovinos

DESTINY IMAGE® PUBLISHERS, INC.

P.O. Box 310, Shippensburg, PA 17257-0310

"Promoting Inspired Lives."

This book and all other Destiny Image, Revival Press, MercyPlace, Fresh Bread, Destiny Image Fiction, and Treasure House books are available at Christian bookstores and distributors worldwide.

For a U.S. bookstore nearest you, call 1-800-722-6774.

For more information on foreign distributors, call 717-532-3040.

Reach us on the Internet: www.destinyimage.com.

ISBN 13 TP: 978-0-7684-0344-2

ISBN 13 Ebook: 978-0-7684-8474-8

For Worldwide Distribution, Printed in the U.S.A.

1 2 3 4 5 6 7 8 / 17 16 15 14 13

DEDICATION

I DEDICATE THIS book to my three life pursuits...

MY GOD:

You have always pursued me.
You have my heart.
This book is all about You.

MY CHRISTELLE LEE:

You are my heavenly pursuit here on earth. You inspire me, teach me, listen to me, and love me. You are my best friend and lover. This book is just as much yours. I'm still fascinated I get to love you with all my heart on this side of heaven. *Tu' Amor.*

MY CHILDREN:

To my children: Michael, Gabriel, Elijah, Isabella, Justice, and Benjamin. You are the crown of my life and the joy of my heart. I desire that you go deeper and further with God than I have ever dreamed. My life is a signpost for you, to the heart of Jesus.

Acknowledgments

I would like to thank:

My parents: Carlos and Sandra Baldovinos for encouraging me and supporting me always and pointing me to Jesus. I will be forever grateful for you. I love you both so much!

My siblings: Carlos and Amy Baldovinos, Marcela and Adam Anderson, and Yoshua Baldovinos. I love you more than you will ever know. It's a great joy for me to have a family that passionately pursues Jesus!

My in-laws and extended family: Mark and Karen Anderson; Sean and Lindsay Anthony; Sean and Kirsten Mark; Jonathan, Cori, and Josiah: I love you all dearly and I have always appreciated your love and support.

The Staff at Global Prayer House: Ryan and Sarah Daw, John and Donna Ross, Mechele Wachnuk, Jacob and Amanda Cook, Wilma Van Niekerk, Braden Scharfenberg, Alexis Norio, Jen Wachnuk, Joel and Melissa Graber, Jordyn Weibe, Joel Stigter, Randi Short, Leslie Rasmussen, Rick and Judy Sorum, Joakim Jansson, Kathy Truer, and the Pursuit Internship and Worship Staff. You are a gift to me and the House of Prayer and the Pursuit vision. I can't imagine anyone else to build a place of His presence with. I love you guys. Thank you for letting me serve you and run with you!

Jeff and Mary Printz: Thank you for your tireless effort in the editing process. I couldn't have done this without you. Your sacrifice truly helped make this book possible.

Kirsten Mark: For your creative expertise and long hours—thank you.

Corey Stark: Your friendship has meant a lot to me over the years. Thank you for your support in this book!

Rick Pino: I love running with you. Keep putting up the tent pegs all over the world! All for Jesus; all for love!

Randy and Deb Pick: Many thoughts and ideas in the message of Relentless Pursuit have been inspired by our long hours of talking and spurring each other on in many of these truths. Thank you for your love and support over the years.

Wes and Janice Reinheller: Over the years you have supported all that I have done and championed God's call on my life. Thank you for your friendship!

God has placed unbelievable friends around my life. I have grown so much through you. I want to acknowledge Jason and Jessica Fluery, Matt and Renee Rood, Merideth Stark, Anna Forsberg, Corey Russell, Sammy Robinson, Tim and Liz Coehoorn, Ken and Alva Klassen, Marlies Wirzba, Aaron and Kendra Melanson, Aaron and Chelsey Wellwood, Sean and Lisa Furlong, Tyler and Melissa Davidson, and Terence and Larissa Kowalchuk, for your friendship and support in the vision that burns on my heart.

CONTENTS

FOREWORD

by Mike Bickle

THE HOLY SPIRIT is inviting us to enjoy intimacy with God by allowing us to experience the deep things of His heart. God's plan is that love would abound on the earth forever. Love is more than just a key thread in the tapestry of the salvation story. It is the main purpose in God's story line that He communicated to Abraham, Moses, David, all the prophets, and His people. And this story line is still being communicated today.

We were created in God's image to be loved and to love on God's terms. The capacity to deeply love is unique to the human spirit, because we are created in the image of God, who is love. The reason we enjoy being loved and loving is because we were made in the image of God, who enjoys loving and being loved.

When our hearts are exhilarated and fascinated with Jesus, we can embrace anything in His will and go anywhere and not rely on status before men. When we know that we are loved by God and when we love Him in response, then we are truly successful. When this truth impacts our heart we are profoundly transformed and awakened to true life as Jesus defines it. This book is an awakening and a taste of what is available if we would just reach for it.

I am encouraged by the ministry at the Global Prayer House Missions Base that Antonio Baldovinos leads. God is using this ministry in a pioneering way, as God brings the House of Prayer movement and the missions movement as one expression under heaven.

In Antonio's book *Relentless Pursuit: Awakening Hearts to Burn for Him,* he gives profound insight into the real and only thing that keeps our heart alive—encountering Jesus Himself.

Through Antonio's personal story you will see how a touch of God on the heart changes everything and can do far more than any ministry effort. We can be in ministry or the marketplace, doing wonderful things for God yet be disconnected with Him in a practical way.

I encourage you to take these truths of prayer, fasting, prioritizing the First Commandment, and devoting yourself in the grace of God to live them out. I believe you will be marked with a vision to go deep in God.

MIKE BICKLE
Founder, International House of Prayer of Kansas City

INTRODUCTION

THE MESSAGE OF *Relentless Pursuit* is not intended to be a "how to" message. *Relentless Pursuit* is much more than a "how to" process. It is a treasure hunt leading to the heart of God. I believe the *Relentless Pursuit* is a prophetic call from His heart to yours.

Throughout this book, I share times in my journey when I was complacent and asleep in my relationship with God. Mine is a great example of how a dull heart can be awakened, and how being revived is only the beginning. I want to burn for Him and continue to be completely alive to the full extent of His grace.

To keep our hearts burning, we must posture our hearts daily in front of the bonfire of His love. That is why I will speak about keys to intimacy, pursuing holiness, living with vision, a life of prayer, and so much more. This book will inspire you; it will help you remove things that hinder love, and it will help you launch your life into experiencing more of His heart. I also share insights on how various leaders throughout the Bible and history lived their lives before the Lord.

God has a plan for you, a destiny that is only yours and yours alone. My prayer as you read my story is that you will be inspired to reach for Him and see that what He did for me is available for you.

No matter what season of life you are in, God sees it all and is waiting with arms open wide for you to respond to His *Relentless Pursuit*. I hope that these stories, practical steps, and tools will catapult you to the heights of all that is available to you on this side of eternity.

ANTONIO BALDOVINOS

Chapter I

THE INVITATION

IN FEBRUARY 2009, I awoke abruptly out of my sleep at three o'clock in the morning. Feeling surprisingly energized and not able to fall back asleep, I decided to get out of bed. As I walked over to the loft where my wife, Christelle, and I spend time praying and reading the Word, I began to wonder why I was wide awake at this time in the morning. I asked God, *"What am I doing here?"* God instantly spoke to my heart and said, *"I'm pursuing you, Antonio."*

My heart stopped for a moment, and I sat there in great amazement. Suddenly I was hit with a life-changing revelation: the Creator of the universe is pursuing *me*.

Moved with great emotion, I began to cry in His presence. In my weak love, I responded to Him. *"I am pursuing You, God."* As I said those words, I felt like I touched His heart, despite my thoughts that my love was infinitely inferior and unworthy of Him.

God instantly responded again, with full assurance, *"I am pursuing you, Antonio."*

This divine dialogue was the first time that I had really realized that God has always been pursuing me. What I had known in my head up until that point now became a reality inside me for the first time. No matter where I went or how far I was from His presence, God had been relentlessly and intensely *pursuing me*.

The height and depth of His love are beyond measure and comprehension. He will go to any measure to have you for Himself. If you don't know this Great Pursuer, let me guarantee you—this great God, the Creator of the heavens and the earth, the Creator of the angels and everything else, is *pursuing you*. The question is: *how are you going to respond to His pursuit of you?*

When we respond to His pursuit, it awakens love for Him in our hearts. Our ability to experience the holiness, magnificence, love, and the glory of God increases. I urge you to go to Him and respond to His pursuit. He will lavish you with love, forgiveness, and joy, and He will completely fulfill you. We are the objects of His tender affections and goodwill. Above all, His goal is intimacy with His people, forever and ever!

DO YOU KNOW HIM?

As you journey through this book, I will lay out pieces of my life story where I started with great zeal to make an impact on the world. It is my calling and destiny to change the earth for the glory of the Lord. I desperately want to make a difference. I'm sure you feel the same way. We all want to leave a mark in history. However, I lived much of my life *doing things* for God instead of *knowing Him*.

> *Not everyone who says to Me, "Lord, Lord," shall enter the kingdom of heaven, but he who does the will of My Father in heaven. Many will say to Me in that day, "Lord, Lord, have we not prophesied in Your name, cast out demons in Your name, and done many wonders in Your name?" And then I will declare to them, "I never knew you;*

depart from Me, you who practice lawlessness!" (Matthew 7:21-23).

I was someone who moved across cities and nations doing things for God but didn't truly *know* Him. You see, you can do things for God and you can even be very successful at it, yet be completely distant from His heart. Matthew 7:21-23 confirms this; it talks about a people who cast out demons, prophesied, and did many wonders in His name. But Jesus simply said to them, *"I don't know you."*

That word *know* means "intimate knowledge." Doing things for people does not equate to knowing or being connected to them. God is not just looking for workers or servants. He is looking for affection-based, intimate lovers who do things out of a deep well of love for Him, not out of duty or fear.

When what we "do" for God comes out of our relationship and love for Him, it isn't hard anymore to put aside our own desires and agendas for His. I agree with Bill Johnson's statement: "The impulse that drives the life of the believer isn't the need to perform for God but to commune with Him."[1] You are most intimate in the natural sense with those you know the best. When I speak about knowing people, it is not just knowing facts about them; it is experiential knowledge of what moves their hearts. The substance of intimacy is growing in the experiential knowledge of a person. Intimacy with God is synonymous with the knowledge of God. As we grow in the experiential knowledge of what He feels and thinks, we grow in intimacy with God.

When my wife and I were courting each other before we were married, she moved to Wisconsin while I still lived in Minnesota. Since long-distance phone calls were so expensive, we chose to write letters to each other. I loved writing about my day and the love I felt for her. And I loved receiving her letters. What made the letters that I received even more special to me, was when she would spray a dab of perfume on each one; and as I read them, it felt like she was there with me.

GOD'S LOVE STORY

The Bible is the greatest love story ever written. It is filled with the history of God's relentless pursuit of His Bride. In reading these words from His heart, they are letters of a Bridegroom to His love, of a lover to His beloved.

The Bible is so much more than words or instructions for life, although it certainly is that; He is releasing His fragrance, His heart's very own passion to us as we read. These words are meant to touch our hearts, transform us, and move us into greater realization of His love and a continual encounter of truly knowing Him. We are meant not just to take in the words, but to take in His aroma of love and drink in His nearness.

In the busyness of our lives, many things distract, deter, and pull for our attention and affections. In the parable of the wise and foolish virgins (see Matt. 25:1-13), we see the emphasis on the need to have a continual, recurrent cultivation of our relationship with Jesus. In this parable we must heed the warning not to become one of the *"foolish"* virgins by neglecting to cultivate intimacy with God.

> *The kingdom...shall be likened to ten virgins who took their lamps and went out to meet the bridegroom. Now five of them were wise, and five were foolish. Those who were foolish took their lamps and took no oil with them, but the wise took oil in their vessels with their lamps* (Matthew 25:1-4).

The foolish took their lamps, which represent ministry; yet they took *"no oil."* They pursued ministry to people instead of acquiring and maintaining the oil of intimacy with God. At one point they were all wise, but the wise can become foolish when they focus on ministry to people (even for sincere reasons) over ministering to God.

The wise virgins *"took oil"* in their lamps, as well as the vessels themselves. The *"oil"* speaks of the presence of God that touches our hearts. So, we see that the wise virgins also did ministry, yet they maintained the oil of intimacy.

> *The foolish said to the wise, "Give us some of your oil for our lamps are going out." The wise answered, saying, "No, lest there should not be enough for us and you; but go rather to those who sell and, buy for yourselves"* (Matthew 25:8-9).

In Matthew 25:8-9 we are exhorted to go and buy oil for ourselves. This is a costly process that no one else can do for us. We cannot have someone else's intimacy with God. We cannot earn this; yet there is a price to pay. The question is: *How do you buy oil?* The answer is you invest your *time.* It takes time to minister to Him to obtain your own oil. The reward far outweighs anything we could ask, think, or imagine. What we are searching for to satisfy all our inner longings is found in one thing: *true intimacy.*

There are inescapable desires that we have within us. We have an innate longing for these desires to be satisfied, and only one thing will ultimately fulfill them—God Himself. Ecclesiastes 3:11 says that *"He has put eternity in their hearts…."* The eternal God created eternal beings and placed eternity in our hearts. Whether we realize it or not, our desire is to be with our eternal God and Father. We desire to know our only satisfaction face to face and heart to heart. It's Him we are looking for—God Himself.

> *So the LORD spoke to Moses face to face, as a man speaks to his friend. And he would return to the camp, but his*

servant Joshua the son of Nun, a young man, did not depart from the tabernacle (Exodus 33:11).

There are some amazing figures throughout the Bible who had face-to-face relationships with God. If you reflect on the fact that Moses spoke to God face to face as a man speaks to his friend, it makes you think, *Wow! How awesome is that?* Not only did Moses desire and get to experience this, but Joshua did also. In fact, when Moses returned to his tent, Joshua stayed in God's presence longer.

JOSHUA GENERATION

I believe that God is raising up such a hunger on earth that not only are we going to have people like Moses who encounter God face to face, but there will also be Joshuas who are going to stay longer. There is a Joshua generation arising that will linger in His presence. They are not staying longer to get a better strategy or plan for the work that has to get done; they deeply desire to encounter the God of their souls. They are staying longer because they know that when we who are eternal encounter eternity Himself, the *I Am,* face to face, we will be awestruck by the fulfillment of every longing, desire, everything we were created for, in that place. This gnawing hunger is only sated by God's touch, and never totally fulfilled. Simply having the merest taste of God or the faintest revelation of Him leaves us knowing there is only One who satisfies, only One who fulfills, only One we've been looking for—Him. All other pleasures barely compare to the awesome pleasure of encountering God.

In Matthew 24:12-13 Jesus says, *"Because of the increase of wickedness, the love of most will grow cold, but he who stands firm to the end will be saved"* (NIV). Friend, the only way to not have your heart grow cold is to have a heart that is awakened with love and hunger for the living God. Then you must contend to maintain and enlarge it.

What matters most is the size of your heart, not the size of your bank account, not your notoriety, ministry, or anything else.

To emphasize my point again, it is the size of your heart that ultimately matters.

God has awakened my heart to the reality of eternity and my eternal longing. I pray that as you read this book you are ignited with passion as you realize God has been more in pursuit of you than you are of Him. *He* is the Great Pursuer, and *we* are responding to His greatest pursuit for our wholehearted love. Join me on this journey and watch as your heart awakens to His *Relentless Pursuit!*

Chapter 2

RELENTLESS PURSUIT

*We pursue God because, and only because, He has first
put an urge within us that spurs us to the pursuit.*
—A.W. TOZER, *The Pursuit of God*

COMING OUT OF the Calgary airport one bitterly cold November morning, I hurried to the car rental kiosk in hopes of avoiding yet another drawn-out wait. After being stuck in an airplane seat for six hours and standing in numerous lines, I was cranky, tired, and irritable. I waited impatiently, and when I finally was handed my car keys, I sighed with relief; at last, no more people and no more delays—or so I thought. I was actually looking forward to my three-hour commute to unwind and relax, undisturbed and by myself.

Five minutes into my drive, I noticed something in the distance—the outline of a young man hitchhiking on the side of the road. I felt that familiar urge of the Lord saying, "Pick him up, Antonio," and I thought, Not now, I'm tired and just want to relax. I knew I should obey, so reluctantly I put on my hazard lights, pulled over, and picked him up. He greeted me with a thankful smile as he began to thaw and shake off the frost from the lengthy time he had spent in the icy chill outside.

With a cordial nod and fake smile, I shook his hand, said hello, and turned the music up louder. He attempted to make conversation, but I remained arrogantly indifferent. After answering his inquiries, I turned the worship music back up. After my continued lack of interest, he finally realized I wasn't in the mood for conversation.

Despite my best efforts to remain detached, I could not ignore the increasing urge within me to speak to this man about what was on God's heart. Suddenly my lack of enthusiasm and selfishness were replaced with conviction and a soberness to do what God wanted. Great compassion and love for the man washed over me; the thought of where he would spend eternity apprehended me. In that moment God began to reveal to me His heart for this man; and in what seemed almost an instant, I turned to my passenger and erupted, "If you were to die today, where would you go?" The young man looked at me, and with shock and full sincerity stammered, "I…I…I don't know. What do you mean?"

"Well," I said, "there is a heaven and there is a hell. You are an eternal being. You will live forever. You will live in heaven or in hell. There is no such thing as paradise, purgatory, limbo, reincarnation, or the like. Heaven was made for you. Hell was not. If you live for God, you will have eternal life. If you don't live for God, you will live forever in hell."

I went on to describe what heaven looked like, and I also described hell. I asked him to grab my Bible from my back seat, and I had him start reading about sin, and what Jesus did on the cross for us concerning our sins. I explained that God wants to have a relationship with us, but sin separates us from having this life of fellowship. I continued to describe how we can have eternal life with God when we exchange our old life for new life in Him. We will have a new life here on Earth with real peace and joy, with the cleansing power over our sin.

After I had explained all of this, the young man's heart was pricked, and he began to unravel his many questions about sin, God, and eternity.

I found that the drive—which I had started out selfishly thinking was never going to end—was now coming to a close. I knew there was not going to be enough time to explain more about God and help the man come into a relationship with Him, so under my breath, I asked the Lord for more time and then proceeded to ask the young hitchhiker his name. He said, "I'm Steve."

I then said, "Steve, I know we are at our destination, but would you join me for lunch?" He earnestly agreed to my invitation.

As I sat down across the table from Steve at an ABC Country restaurant, hoping that all I had said was sinking in, he shocked me by saying that he had been hitchhiking for the past three days and that during those three days, *every driver* in *every car* he had been in had talked to him about God and eternity!

I was dumbfounded. I now knew that God was aggressively *pursuing* Steve. God delighted in him and wanted him so much that He had numerous drivers share this with Steve over a three-day period! Our conversation continued and our lunchtime couldn't have lasted long enough.

As the plates were being cleared, I began to think of a way to get more time with Steve. I volunteered to take him a little bit farther, even though it was well out of my way. I needed more time. I knew God was pursuing him with great urgency, and I had an intense burning within me to bring Steve to a place of response after three days of God's relentless pursuit.

We walked outside to the rental car, sat down, and not being able to contain it any longer, I turned to Steve and blurted out, "Steve, God is after you. He loves you and wants to know you. And He wants you to know Him. He is calling you with great urgency and desperation. I want you to know how much He loves you. He has been trying to get your attention."

I then closed my eyes, raised my voice, and with as much passion and affection as I could, I screamed out the words I felt straight from the Lord: *"Steve, Steve, I love you and I want to be with you. I want you to be with Me. I love you. I gave My life for you. Would you lay down your life and take My life? I love you."*

I opened my eyes and looked at Steve. He turned to me with tears rolling down his face, and with a look of great joy and hungry desperation he said, "Yes, I want Him." My heart leapt and gratefulness filled my whole being with the goodness of God and how much He loves us!

I tell you this story because just like Steve, God is passionately pursuing all of us. I believe God is aggressively and fervently pursuing you—no matter where you are in life. He loves you. He loves you so much and wants nothing else but for a voluntary love response from you to Him.

INTENSE PURSUIT

"We love Him because He first loved us" (1 John 4:19). God's pursuit begins before salvation for everyone; before we ever get introduced to Jesus or even to who God is or what He's done for us. God has been relentlessly pursuing you, and no matter where you find yourself in this journey be assured of this: God loves *you*. God has done everything possible to have a real and true relationship with you. His love is constant and never fades, fails, or ends. Moreover, God will continue to fervently chase you down to have this relationship with you.

> *Or do you think Scripture says without reason that he jealously longs for the spirit he has caused to dwell in us?* (James 4:5 NIV).

God longs to have a vibrant and true relationship with us. The New King James translation of this verse says that He *"yearns jealously."* I know this thought doesn't really go through our minds or our hearts when it comes to our relationship with God. We think of longing and envious desire for boyfriends or girlfriends, husbands or wives, but don't often imagine God desiring *us* like that.

I think this is partly the case because many Christians don't think He really loves them. If you are one of them, let me assure you, God loves you. His love is boundless, limitless, and intensely jealous. He is jealous over us and He will not share us with anyone or anything. He wants us to be solely His.

I'm frequently captivated by the thought of God sending His Son Jesus to die on the cross for each one of us. He died on the cross because sin separated us from relationship. He removed any obstacle in the way of a possible relationship with us.

> *For God so loved the world that He gave His only begotten Son, that whoever believes in Him should not perish but have everlasting life* (John 3:16).

Everlasting life is made possible through Jesus' sacrifice. God loved us so much, He sent His only Son to die on the cross, so that nothing would separate us from Him anymore. What an act of love and sacrifice.

My question is *why?* Why would Jesus do this? Why would Jesus die on the cross for our sins?

> *And being found in appearance as a man, He humbled Himself and became obedient to the point of death, even the death of the cross* (Philippians 2:8).

Why would Jesus take on the form of a human being and obey to the point of death? Even though this is an unimaginable thought that Jesus would obey His Father even to death, what was the *motive* for Jesus to give His life?

...Jesus... for the joy that was set before Him endured the
cross... (Hebrews 12:2).

On top of laying His life down in full obedience, Jesus endured
the cross with and for great joy. Why?

Let me suggest that Jesus not only died on the cross as an obedient Son, but as a Lover. He loves us so intensely, that He will not
allow anything to come in between Him and us. Consequently, there
is truly no mountain too high, no valley too low, and no sacrifice so
great that He would not give up His life, with great joy.

And He did. His motive was twofold. One was as an obedient
Son, to His father, but the even greater reason was because He loves
you that much. Jesus died and gave up His life as a Lover of God and
a Lover of *us*.

God's greatest desire for His creation is to have a family for
Himself and a Bride for His Son. This was the ultimate purpose
for creation. When I read the Bible, I realize that everything is
about a wedding; the Bible begins and ends in a wedding. God
is preparing a Bride for His Son. Our lives are really about our
encountering Him as the Bridegroom (see Matt. 25:1). The Father
set His heart to compel and inspire the Bride to prepare herself to
be with Jesus.

...for the marriage of the Lamb has come, and His wife
has made herself ready (Revelation 19:7).

God is preparing His Bride to be ready, and His relentless pursuit
is to know and have relationship with us even now.

Now, let me pause for a second to clarify something. For some
men, it might be difficult to imagine the concept that they are the
Bride of Christ. Let me put it this way: throughout the Bible, just
as women are referred to as the "sons of God," men are also referred
to as the "Bride of Christ." The Bible is speaking about our *position*

rather than gender. It is referring to our position of proximity to the heart of God.

We have three main identities: 1) as servants and friends (through whom the gifts of the Holy Spirit flow), 2) as sons of God (sharing a relationship of affection with the Father, as well as authority), and 3) the Bride of Christ (enjoying closeness to His heart and partnership with Jesus).

These three main identities complement each other and reflect who we are. They should never be confused with gender, but rather define our positional identity in relation to the Godhead. Let's continue...

UNCEASING PURSUIT

Mike Bickle's teaching series, *Studies in the Bride of Christ,* helped shape many of my own thoughts on this powerful subject.[1] Let's take a deeper look into what it means to be the Bride of Christ, as the life story of Hosea so powerfully illustrates.

In the Book of Hosea we find the incredible story of God commanding Hosea to marry a prostitute named Gomer. God's people at this time had been living in deep spiritual adultery. God was instructing Hosea to marry a prostitute so that Hosea would experience the pain that God was experiencing. God wanted Hosea's marriage to be a prophetic picture of the way God felt in regard to Israel.

> When the LORD began to speak by Hosea, the LORD said to Hosea: "Go, take yourself a wife of harlotry and children of harlotry, for the land has committed great harlotry by departing from the LORD" (Hosea 1:2).

We find Hosea's story described in chapters one through three, where God also charged Israel with marital unfaithfulness and prophetically compared Hosea's unfaithful wife to the nation (see Hos. 2:2-13).

God wanted Hosea to experience the pain, disappointment, and joy of the recovery of a broken marriage relationship. This equipped Hosea to be the first prophet to make known the Bridegroom God to Israel and the nations.

THORNS BRING US BACK

Even though this can be hard for us to comprehend, God uses difficult circumstances and trials in our lives to draw us to Him. God desires all of us. He doesn't want our hearts, minds, affections, or our strength to be given to anyone or anything except to Him. So He will use whatever it takes to draw us and bring us to Him.

> *Therefore, behold, I will hedge up your way with thorns, and wall her in, so that she cannot find her paths. She will chase her lovers...she will seek them, but not find them. Then she will say, "I will go and return to my first husband, for then it was better for me than now"* (Hosea 2:6-7).

Hosea's message was new in two ways: first, in introducing the Lord as a Bridegroom God, a God with great desire; then secondly, in saying that the northern kingdom would be destroyed within one generation. The message was that a Bridegroom God orchestrated and manifested both judgment and restoration.

Hosea loved his nation and his wife, so he suffered greatly. His message was given just before severe judgment came on the northern kingdom of Israel. Israel experienced civil war in 931 B.C. For about two hundred years (931–721 B.C.), Israel was divided. Hosea prophesied to the north during a time of economic prosperity. This was the first time that the "Bride of Christ" message was declared to Israel, and it was given in the context of judgment. Only by understanding His heart as a Bridegroom can we interpret His judgments.

The One who judges loves so much that He will remove *all* that hinders love.

Israel forgot, but God will pursue her until she loves Him. Jesus will draw Israel to Himself, just like He does you and me, no matter where we are in our journey, even if we have forgotten Him. He uses both the judgment of thorns and the allurement of His kindness and beauty (see Hos. 2:6-7;14) to have a relationship with us.

> *...But Me she forgot....Therefore...I will allure her, will bring her into the wilderness, and speak comfort to her.... She shall sing there...as in the day when she came up from...Egypt* (Hosea 2:13-15).

ALLURE

God's main way of turning us from unfaithfulness is by His kindness and beauty. It's His kindness that leads us to repentance (see Rom. 2:4). That is what turns our hearts toward Him. Also, once we see His character, His heart, and His majesty, our hearts become enamored of His beauty. God's greatest quality is being powerfully and mysteriously attractive or fascinating to us. If we turn our gaze toward Him, His beauty enraptures us. The revelation of God's beauty and kindness deeply touches the human spirit (see Isa. 4:2).

SHE SHALL SING THERE

In the Book of Hosea, God awakens Israel with new songs, even in her wilderness struggles. I have seen this in my own life. God has used struggle or difficulty to get my attention and eventually my heart. I have several friends who have even come to follow Jesus due to some difficult situation where they cried out to Him: "God help!"

God wants our emotional and physical reach to be toward Him. This is one of the main reasons why prayer in communion with the uncreated God is so powerful, and truly a miracle. *"You do not have because you do not ask"* (James 4:2).

God wants us to talk to Him. God knows all of our needs (see Matt. 6:32), but requires that we ask for them because it causes us to interact with His heart. To ask implies that we verbalize and meditate on our prayers, not just think on them. One foundational principle of the kingdom is that we ask God for everything, both the increase of good things and the decrease of bad things. Prayer does not earn us God's favor, but positions us to receive more by relationship that is engaging in active intimacy with God.

RELENTLESS PURSUIT IS OUT OF LOVE

To summarize this chapter I will end by saying, "He is relentlessly pursuing you." As mentioned previously, Hebrews 12:2 talks about the joy set before Him. I'm convinced that the joy that was set before Him is Isaiah 62:5: *"As a bridegroom rejoices with great joy over his bride, so God rejoices over you"* (NIV, paraphrased).

The rejoicing, the joy set before Him, was the obtaining of His Bride. When His Bride rebels and turns her heart away from Him, it brings significant pain to His heart. Nevertheless, He loves His Bride so much, even in the midst of pain; He endured the cross for her. He simply has to have you. *This* is relentless love. *This* is *Relentless Pursuit.*

IGNITING A HEART

I have one desire now—to live a life of
reckless abandon for the Lord, putting
all my energy and strength into it.
—ED MCCULLY, quoted in *Through Gates of Splendor*

FOCUSED. BUSY. SUCCESSFUL. These are all words that described my life before being ignited with the fire of the Holy Spirit and tasting the love of God. I started out full of zeal climbing a ladder of success in Christian ministry. I wanted to make an impact and leave a mark. My zeal and passion were not completely wrong. I was simply misdirected. I believe there is a generation that God is raising up, fully abandoned for one purpose and one aim—Him.

> ...*I am your shield, your exceedingly great reward*
> (Genesis 15:1).

For more than ten years, I traveled to many cities around the world organizing and facilitating evangelistic campaigns. It was a great delight knowing that my energy and strength were being spent toward people responding to Jesus. I have seen tens of thousands of people say "yes" to following Him.

Slowly however, I began to get busier, and my heart began to get dull. My focus began to slightly change and turn. At the pinnacle of my so-called "success," I became a professional Christian minister, focusing my attention and affections on what I did, how many people attended our meetings, how much money was being raised, and how many people I could lead and influence.

I don't want to give the wrong impression. I don't see anything wrong with success or large meetings. Each of us has been created to make an impact, a big impact. What I want to challenge is the reason. Why do we want to make an impact? What is the motivation of our hearts?

I also want to ask you two questions. Do you live your life out of fullness? Are you fully alive in God?

We all have different pursuits. We have pursuits of success, fame, wealth, and other temporal quests. Some have significance, but most have very little weight in the perspective of life and eternity.

The real question is *do we know Him*? He is our exceedingly great reward. He is our only satisfaction. He is what we are really longing to capture and take a hold of. God is placing the first commandment back in first place, by zealously pursuing us. This is what He did in my heart.

Slowly over time, my love for God began to grow cold and the love that had overflowed into zeal for souls became a Christian business mentality. It was no longer something I did out of passion for Him and people, but something I did only because it was "the good thing to do" and I became very skilled at it. I remember one time being at my own event and feeling the conviction of the Holy Spirit to respond to the altar call myself. I was too afraid of what others would think, and chose not to go. That resulted in a heart that grew even more callous toward God. Thankfully, God would not take my *no* for an answer and He continued to pursue me, woo me, call me, time and again.

We serve a God who has great zeal and unwavering desire for us. He is jealous for our time, affections, and aspirations. It was with this great desire and His great mercy that He seized my heart for Him.

We were designed to have deep intimacy with Him, to be fascinated with Him, to walk with Him. When we touch, taste, feel, hear, and see Him we know what it means to be truly alive. When these God longings are not filled, we search to fill the empty space. Inevitably, we come up short.

It has been since God arrested my heart again that my passion to awaken people to Him has increased to levels beyond anything I ever experienced before. Once I tasted Him, I had to share Him with everyone around me. This great love is the ingredient to reaching the lost and awakening the Church. A lover will always go further and harder than a worker or a servant. Lovers do not count the cost or weigh the price; they just do it out of desire for the one they love. When we become servants and workers before lovers, it is only a matter of time before our hearts will grow cold. When we become lovers of God, this zeal for people becomes a reality that makes any mountain, trial, or effort seem small in light of knowing Him.

FIRST LOVE

> *Jesus said to him "You shall love the LORD your God with all your heart, with all your soul, and with all your mind. This is the first and great commandment. And the second is like it: You shall love your neighbor as yourself"* (Matthew 22:37-39).

The command to love God with our heart, soul, and mind is the first and greatest commandment. Many live their lives doing the second commandment first; serving, winning the lost, discipling, etc.

This is all necessary. I am not saying this isn't love. For the most part, however, the second commandment has become the primary focus where many put most of their energy, attention, and affection.

Yet, God is reprioritizing this in people's lives. Thank God He did this in my life. I became distracted, discontented, and was really just going through the motions of loving God—with no heart reality of knowing Him. Now I am consistently reminding myself and resigning myself to my real heart's cry and desire; to love God with everything in me.

The first commandment is premiere to God, the first priority in the kingdom, and the chief emphasis of the Holy Spirit. It's the great commandment. Many view this as an option but it's not; it's a command from God Himself. It is the commandment that has the greatest force on God's heart, the greatest effect on our hearts, the greatest impact on the people whom we serve, and has been considerably overlooked and dismissed by the Body of Christ throughout history. Loving God is an end in itself, not the way to something else.

There are two words in Matthew 22:37—*first* and *great*—that are of enormous importance. These words have the greatest meaning for our lives and for this generation. We can't reduce these words to casual statements. These two words have extreme weight.

The first commandment reveals God's primary purpose for creation, His eternal motivation. From before the foundation of the world, God had a plan in His heart. Before the world was, He had a reason behind what He did. He has a reason behind everything He does. We know what happened: He created the heavens and the earth. He created us. We know what He did on the cross: He redeemed us because sin had separated us. He did it so we could be with Him. Matthew 22:37 shows us what the most important instruction is for how to live our lives. In summary, God simply wants to establish a family for Himself. As a father myself, I completely understand this.

As I stated in the previous chapter, God is raising up faithful children, sons and daughters who are loyal to Him in love; and He is also raising up a Bride for His Son who will be His companion for eternity. God's ultimate eternal purpose for creation is this: "God wanted to establish a family for Himself. He wanted to raise up faithful children, sons and daughters who would be loyal to Him in love, and He also wanted to raise up an equally-yoked Bride for His Son who would be His eternal companion. The Father promised His Son an inheritance. That inheritance is a people whom He would totally possess. Jesus' inheritance involves more than real estate, more than owning the nations, more than government, more than the fact that He controls the nations..."[1] —it is you and me, His people.

OBEDIENCE AND VOLUNTARY LOVE

Jesus' inheritance involves the required obedience of all creation. In Philippians 2:10-11, Paul gives us some insight: the Father promises that every knee will bow, every tongue will confess, every demon in hell will bow down their knees in obedience. Every unbeliever, when assigned eternal judgment, will go there in obedience to the Word of Jesus.

Obedience of all creation is required, but there is so much more to God's heart. God wants more than required obedience. He wants voluntary love. The inheritance of the King is the obedience of all the nations, but the inheritance of the Bridegroom is the voluntary love of all the people in all the nations. As a King, He receives His inheritance: "Every knee will bow." As a Bridegroom, He receives an inheritance: "Every heart in Your kingdom will love You." All of the redeemed will love Him. Not dictated, not forced, not programmed; it will be voluntary love! They will choose to love God because they will see Him and they will want Him. To obey God is to love Him (see John 14:15).

When we begin to see Him for who He is, we not only desire to please Him, but we begin to see sin as an obstruction to getting closer to Him. Jesus paid the price to wipe away our sin so that we have unhindered access to Him and the Father. When we set our hearts in sincerity to be obedient to the Lord and make quality decisions to pursue righteousness, we *will* sin less and less, because He will help us. When we set our hearts to obey Him, we are saying, "I love you," which moves His heart and He responds with, "I love you" every time.

THE DESIRE OF JESUS

I am gripped with a portion of Scripture that I pray, as you read it, will mark your heart with the reality of how much Jesus desires you.

Before Jesus died on the cross, He prayed what is called the High Priestly Prayer. The crescendo of His prayer is found at the end of John 17. I want you to capture His heart as you read this. There is nothing like this prayer in the entire Bible—Jesus is praying for His glorious Bride. The manner in which this prayer ends is a volcanic explosion that directly precedes His going to the garden. In other words, this prayer and desire of Jesus contain His final thoughts and one of His last requests to God as He went to the cross. The prayer expresses His very motives and heartbeat for dying: to be with us.

> *Father, I desire that they also whom You gave Me may be with Me where I am, that they may behold My glory which you have given Me; for you loved Me before the foundation of the world. O righteous Father! The world has not known You, but I have known You; and these have known that You sent Me. And I have declared to them Your name, and will declare it, that the love with*

which You loved Me may be in them, and I in them
(John 17:24-26).

Recently I was in Myanmar, South Asia, with our Pursuit Internship students, a five-month discipleship school at Global Prayer House. As I was preparing and going over the teaching I was going to present, I felt prompted by the Holy Spirit to read John 17. As I began to read and meditate on these verses, the reality of His prayer struck me. Here we find Jesus consumed with extravagant passion as He starts this prayer with the words: *"I desire."* Please don't take these two words lightly or skim over them. These powerful words display heart-rending emotion of the greatest kind.

Jesus knew He was about to die on the cross, yet all He could think about was His desire for us. He was filled with burning passion as He laid down His life for His beloved Bride. He was fiercely and jealously consumed with desire over us. This was not casual love, this was costly life-surrendering love because He desired one thing—us. Jesus asked His Father that those who love Him could be with Him where He is. He passionately prayed that the love that He has, feels, and knows from the Father would be given to us. Jesus desired that we would feel and know that same love. God is capturing the Church with this love.

My heart is so moved with this reality. Even as I read this Scripture passage, I pray, "Yes, give it to me, God. I want to know the Father the way Jesus knows Him. I want to know this kind of love. Holy Spirit I ask that You reveal the Father to me, like Jesus knows Him." This has now become my desire, and I pray that it becomes yours, too.

What an amazing picture of the motivation of God's heart. The Father has a worthy Son; and He is raising up a Bride, a ready Bride. God is raising up a generation in which the Bride is made ready by voluntary love, by the supernatural presence of the Holy Spirit who will restore the first commandment to first place.

LIVING OUT OF THE OVERFLOW

*And the second is like it: You shall love your neighbor as
yourself* (Matthew 22:39).

When we follow the first commandment (to love God with all
of our heart), the second commandment (to love our neighbors) will
overflow out of this. It is unthinkable to separate these two commandments. All who love God with all of their hearts will love people
because that is God's nature. Their hearts will be inflamed; they will
love people far more and far better. Their motivations will be placed
correctly. They will not be easily offended. They will not "burn out"
or get tired out. I'm not talking about getting physically tired, necessarily; I am talking about our hearts being fully alive. This is how we
are destined to live.

Which is more important; the first commandment or the second
commandment? The first comes in sequence because the first is what
empowers us for the second. If you are pursing the second commandment without first pursuing the first commandment, you will end up
bankrupt in your ability to sustain it. You need a fresh encounter of
love from God and *love to* Him in order to pour out love to others.
You can't give out what you don't have. It is impossible to love God
without loving what He loves—people. You will always love believers
and unbelievers if you love God.

HOW DO WE LOVE HIM?

There is much discussion today about God's love. There is also
much discussion about how to love God in response. Many view loving God with a distorted view of God's grace. Many think you don't
have to do anything in pursuing to love God. Many view their time
in a worship service, singing songs as their response to His love. These
things express love to God, that's true. Jesus however, defined loving

Him as being deeply embedded in a spirit of obedience (see John 14:21). There is no such thing as loving God without setting ourselves to obey His Word.

> *If you love Me, keep My commandments….He who has My commandments and keeps them, it is he who loves Me….If anyone loves Me, he will keep My word…"* (John 14:15,21,23).

We must love God the way He desires love, not the way we think we should love. We cannot define loving God according to our human culture that seeks love without regarding obedience to God's Word. Jesus wants love from us that allows Him to consume our lives. There are many definitions of love in the culture of the Church today; but we should want to define our love according to Scripture.

Love is more than a commitment to obey God in a general way. We must contend for a sustained "reach" for full obedience. When we sin, we repent and renew our resolve to reach to fully obey with a confidence that God enjoys us in the process. The Lord values our journey to grow in love. We are equally joined to Jesus not by the size of our love, but by the "all" of our love. Though our all may be small, the point is that it is our all. I am so thankful for this.

A heart set to full obedience, as I will talk about further in a later chapter, "includes bridling our speech (see James 3:2), making a covenant with our eyes that refuse to look on anything that stirs up lust (see Job 31:1), disciplining our physical appetites, and managing our time (for service and prayer) and our finances to increase the kingdom."[2] We love God on His terms, with a heart fully aimed at obeying Him because we love Him, because we *get to*. It is our greatest privilege to love Him according to His definition.

We obey because we love. Obedience can often have a negative connotation. It seems like God is a dictator who controls love by submission to obedience. There is a better way to view our obedience to

God and that *is agreement with God's heart.* This is affection-based obedience, which is love. It is fueled by passion because God's grace sustains our love. This is not fear-based obedience. We want to live our lives in affection-based obedience because we love Him and He loves us. We want to live a life that is in agreement with the heart of God; this is real freedom.

God is raising up a people who love Him passionately, with full abandonment. There is a company of people who are after God's heart—a people in one accord with His heart who love what He loves and hate what He hates. Together let's be those people!

Chapter 4

KNOWING GOD

I would rather pay the price to hear God's
voice personally, regardless of how difficult the
circumstances may be, than to have to settle for always
hearing from Him secondhand.
—Joy Dawson, *Forever Ruined for the Ordinary*

A T 6' 6" and weighing 195 pounds, "Air Jordan," as he was called, left an imprint on the game of basketball forever. As a five-time league Most Valuable Player, ten-time scoring champion, and six-time finals champion, Michael Jordan finished his career with 32,292 points and a career average of 30.12 points per game, which is the best in National Basketball Association history. He is still considered to be the best basketball player ever.

After Michael joined his high school team, as a tenth grader, he was cut from the varsity team. This pushed him to work hard and eventually excel to become the greatest basketball player of all time. I could go on and on and tell you everything there is to know about Michael Jordan. As a teenage basketball player and enthusiast, I was familiar with every move, statistic, and accomplishment that Michael ever achieved. I could tell you all *about* Michael Jordan, but I didn't *know* him at all. I have never even met him; and furthermore, he doesn't know me.

I am overwhelmingly grateful that one of the most intriguing mysteries about God is that He not only knows *everything* about us, but He knows us better than we know ourselves.

> *O LORD, You have searched me and known me. You know my sitting down and my rising up; You understand my thought afar off. You comprehend my path and my lying down, and are acquainted with all my ways. For there is not a word on my tongue, but behold, O LORD, You know it altogether. You have hedged me behind and before, and laid Your hand upon me. Such knowledge is too wonderful for me; it is high, I cannot attain it* (Psalm 139:1-6).

How awesome and mind-boggling is the reality revealed in Psalm 139? He knows me that much and wants to be with me all day long. He is watching me day and night. His ears are attentive to my every word, even my every thought. I tell my kids all the time that God can't wait to speak to them all day long.

He *longs* to hear from us. He wants a talking and walking relationship with us day and night. God desires to talk to us about everything in our lives. His interest goes beyond the details of our lives; He's after every aspect of our heart. He is the all-consuming God!

> *Then the man and his wife heard the sound of the LORD God as he was walking in the garden in the cool of the day...* (Genesis 3:8 NIV).

God created us for His pleasure. He formed us so that we can have divine communion with Him and enjoy sweet and mysterious interactions with Him all day. After all, we were made in His image.

He meant for us to see Him and live with Him and draw our life from Him. Adam and Eve walked with God in the cool of the day. What an unfathomable reality: speaking *face to face* with the Creator of the universe is an incredible thought!

My life has been greatly impacted by A.W. Tozer's teachings, specifically by his book, *The Pursuit of God*.[1] Here are some thoughts for you to consider. We have been guilty of "rebellion." In this guilt we have fled as far away as possible from Him and His presence. Instead of running to Him, we ran away from Him. Yet, who can really flee from His presence? Adam tried to flee from His presence when He sinned, and even Peter withdrew from Jesus when he cried at His feet, *"Depart from me, for I am a sinful man, O Lord!"* (Luke 5:8).

Thereafter, man's life upon the earth was separated from His presence, torn apart from that blissful anchor, which is our right and proper dwelling place and what He originally intended for us. This state of being apart from God is what has caused our unceasing restlessness within our hearts and with life. There is an intense cry and unsatisfied longing in people that makes them want more. All over the world people want to experience and live in the fullness that was intended for them from the very beginning. The desperate cry is to know God. There is one reason for this desperation: *nothing* else satisfies except Him. He is our exceedingly great reward. We were created to know the uncreated God.

The whole redemptive work of God is to undo the tragic effects of our rebellion, and to bring us back again into right and eternal relationship with Him. This requires our sins to be disposed of once and for all, and that we live in His presence as before. As David powerfully wrote: *"As far as the east is from the west, so far has He removed our transgressions from us"* (Ps. 103:12). Now that God has really taken care of our sins, when our restless heart feels a yearning for the presence of God, it only requires a response from us. God is calling us to spend time with Him. *"My heart has heard you say, 'Come and talk with me.' And my heart responds, 'LORD, I am coming'"* (Psalm 27:8 NLT).

KNOWING GOD

I have traveled to many cities around the world. Throughout my travels I have worked and spoken in hundreds of churches and I have seen one common deficiency: the lack of *knowing God and His presence.* The world is perishing because of the extreme lack of the knowledge of God, and the Church is starving because of the lack of His presence. The cure for most of our religious mindsets would be to enter into His presence in spiritual experience, drink deep, and to become fully aware that we are in God and He is in us.

The Bible describes the fact that men and women can know God to the same degree that they know any other person or thing in this world. The same terminology used for describing our physical senses, is used to express the knowledge of God throughout the Bible, such as the following examples:

> *Oh, taste and see that the LORD is good...* (Psalm 34:8).

> *All Your garments are scented with myrrh and aloes and cassia, out of the ivory palaces, by which they have made You glad* (Psalm 45:8).

> *My sheep hear My voice, and I know them, and they follow Me* (John 10:27 NASB).

> *Blessed are the pure in heart, for they shall see God* (Matthew 5:8).

There are many additional passages throughout the Bible that describe and express how we can know God in a tangible way, with our own understanding. God wants to reveal Himself to us in even greater ways than these. These are just the elementary and foundational ways of knowing Him. We become familiar with our five senses by exercising them in our physical world. In the same manner we have within us spiritual senses; we can use them to know God and the spiritual world if we will obey the Spirit's urge and begin to exercise them.

To confirm my earlier observation of the Church, I have noticed one sad statement I keep hearing from Christians from various gatherings and meetings. People say something like, *"I give financially. I attend church. But I don't really know God."* My question is why do the redeemed children of God know so little about the reality of communion with God that the Bible clearly states we can and should have?

The answer: our chronic unbelief. Faith enables our spiritual senses to function. Where faith is missing or lacking, the result will be inward numbness toward spiritual things. This is the sad and unnecessary condition that a vast number of Christians face today.

APPETITES

As I watch people's patterns of life and ways of living, I am truly horrified by what our society feeds on. As we increase our intake of earthly entertainment, we dull our capacity to know God. It's not that we don't want to know God; it's that we are too full from eating the lesser things of entertainment, that we can't see God or taste God when He's right in front of us. We are indulging ourselves with so many hours of television, internet, and secular music that God Himself is not given room to whisper to us, to reveal Himself and show us who He is.

Moreover, entertainment is not only dissatisfying us, but it is also destroying us. The enemy, to lull us to sleep, uses these temporal forms of entertainment. The result is that God cannot move in our lives and so the Creator of the universe cannot show Himself to us. Most people are feeding themselves with a steady diet of entertainment that has numbed and deadened them to the reality of God.

One of the greatest problems facing the Body of Christ today is that of spiritual boredom. Many churches are made up of people who have been inundated with entertainment and recreation. All week long they are fully engaged and locked into media of all sorts. Pastors feel compelled to compete with the things that grapple for the attention of their church attendees. A night out at the latest blockbuster movie can move us to tears, but the worship service the next morning does nothing to get our attention. We are dulled into expecting temporal and worldly fulfillment, rather than devoting ourselves to fascination with the eternal. It is tragic how we invest what limited passion we have in things that simply do not satisfy.

SPIRITUAL ANOREXIA

Stephen Arterburn and Debra Cherry bring to light the reality of our spiritual anorexia from their book, *Feeding Your Appetites:*

> Although we have a natural, innate appetite for God and spiritual things, we may not be experiencing the sensations that would tell us we are hungering for Him. Why not? Maybe it's because we have been depriving ourselves of spiritual food for way too long. Are you refusing to feed yourself spiritually? If you don't actively seek God and instead ignore this yearning from deep inside, cravings can, and do, eventually change.
>
> When we are physically hungry, our body sends us signals through our hunger pangs and cravings that tell us we need to eat. If ignored, these signals at first grow stronger in hopes of pushing us to fulfill the need for food. But if we continue to ignore this appetite for long enough, it will eventually begin to fade and we can actually convince ourselves that we really aren't hungry anymore. That is exactly what the anorexic does. She tells herself she isn't hungry

and ignores the signals her body is sending her. Eventually she will have completely numbed her cravings to the point that she no longer desires food. She has so effectively convinced herself that she is not hungry, that her body is now starving to death. Yet she doesn't even realize the danger. So too when we squelch our hunger for God.

This is how it can be with our spiritual appetite. When we are spiritually hungry, we experience the beckoning of the Holy Spirit within us to feast on the things of God. If we ignore our craving for God long enough, we will find the craving for Him eventually begins to fade. We are capable of convincing ourselves that we are doing "just fine," yet we are starving our spirit to the point of spiritual death. Our desires for the things of God fade, and we are no longer able to experience the draw of the Holy Spirit because we have so numbed ourselves to His call. Without even noticing it, prayer has become less important, we no longer thirst after God's Word, and we convince ourselves it's no big deal to miss church.

Both types of anorexics refuse themselves the nourishment they need to sustain life. The only way for both of them to heal and regain a healthy appetite that will help them grow is to pull up to the table and eat. Are you feasting at the banquet table of God? If you want to cultivate and grow your spiritual craving, you must feed it. Psalm 34:8 says, "Taste and see that the Lord is good." When you come to the banquet table to feast on the things of the Spirit, you will find that the Lord is good and that He satisfies completely. And, although the Lord does completely satisfy, once you taste of Him, you will find yourself wanting more and more of Him.[2]

REALITY OF GOD

God is real. He is real in the absolute and final sense that *nothing* else is. All other reality is contingent upon Him, not on what we feel or think. The great reality is God. And no matter what the world tries to offer or tell us, God and the spiritual world are real. Spiritual things are there (or instead we should say *here*) inviting our attention and challenging our trust.

> *...For the things which are seen are temporary, but the things which are not seen are eternal* (2 Corinthians 4:18).

Our trouble is that we have established bad thought patterns. We habitually think of the visible world as real and doubt the reality of any other. We do not deny the existence of the spiritual world, but we doubt that it is really real in the accepted meaning of the word. The real existence of the spirit world is proven by a great story that pulls away the curtain to reveal what we do not see.

Allow me to illustrate this. Elisha, a prophet of God, had made a neighboring nation enraged by warning Israel when the enemy's army was going to attack them. God instructed Elisha time and again and King Aram would be too late to attack every time. The King finally planned to attack and take care of Elisha. He went at night, while everyone was sleeping and set up his army surrounding Elisha. And then here's what it says in the Bible in Second Kings:

> *And when the servant of the man of God arose early and went out, there was an army, surrounding the city with horses and chariots. And his servant said to him, "Alas, my master! What shall we do?" So he answered, "Do not fear, for those who are with us are more than those who are with them." And Elisha prayed, and said, " LORD, I pray, open his eyes that he may see." Then the LORD opened*

*the eyes of the young man, and he saw. And behold, the
mountain was full of horses and chariots of fire all around
Elisha* (2 Kings 6:15-17).

The conclusion is remarkable. The story vividly gives us a glimpse
into true spiritual reality. It's more than what we see, hear, feel, taste,
and touch. Spiritual reality is more real than what we know. What
many don't realize is that we could live in this reality today, but there
is an assault against our living in and comprehending the spiritual
world and its relativity to us.

The natural world intrudes upon our attention day and night for
all of our lives. It is persuasive, determined, and self-destructive. It
does not appeal to our faith; instead, it bombards us through our
five senses, demanding to be accepted as real and final. But sin also
has clouded the lenses of our hearts so that we cannot see the other,
true reality: the City of God, shining around us. The sensory world
triumphs time and again. The visible becomes the enemy of the invis-
ible, and the temporal the enemy of the eternal. That is the tragic
curse inherited by every member of Adam's race.

Our natural reality tends to make contrasts between the spiritual
and the real; but no such contrasts actually exist. The spiritual is
undeniably real.

THE CALL TO ABANDONMENT

I want to call you to live in the fullness of God. The grace of God
calls us to total abandonment, not only because God is worthy of our
undivided attention, but because total abandonment is the *only* way
our spirit becomes alive and energized toward Him. It's not just that
God is worthy of our being wholehearted; it's the only way we can
live safely. That's how the human heart is made: if we have nothing
worth dying for, we have nothing worth living for. If we don't have a
cause to which we give everything, we become bored with life.

We need an awakening. We need our eyes to be opened so that we can finally, actually *see* God. Our desperate cry and our hunger can begin to be fulfilled today. Just as Elisha asked God to open up the eyes of his assistant, the eyes of his understanding, I want to ask God to reveal the spiritual world around us—but even more than that, to open up our eyes so that we can see Him! I want to encourage you to pray this prayer and to continually pray this prayer…

> *I keep asking that the God of our Lord Jesus Christ, the glorious Father, may give you the Spirit of wisdom and revelation, so that you may know him better. I pray also that the eyes of your heart may be enlightened in order that you may know the hope to which he has called you, the riches of his glorious inheritance in his holy people, and his incomparably great power for us who believe.* (Ephesians 1:17-19 NIV).

Our greatest need is to receive a greater measure of the Spirit of wisdom and revelation. This is almost always the greatest need of your loved ones (saved and unsaved), ministries, cities, nations, or governments that you pray for. Satan's most common weapon is the opposite of this; he attacks by releasing accusation and deception to confuse our hearts and close our spiritual eyes.

Let's examine these verses in Ephesians 1 in more depth:

Our eyes being enlightened, explains what it means to receive the Spirit of wisdom and revelation. In other words, our minds are enabled to perceive God and God imparts grace to our affections to love God and feel His presence.

That you may know, (experience)—to know is to encounter and experience God's glory.

Revelation is the unveiling of God Himself. Here is further definition of the word *know* or *knowledge* in this verse:

1. The Greek word *knowledge* is *epignosis* and refers to divine or true knowledge; it is to know something more strongly and clearly than you did before. It is more intense than just to know. It is informational knowledge as well as experiential; it is a continual unveiling.

2. To know or encounter God is what eternal salvation is all about. *"This is eternal life, that they may **know You,** the only true God, and Jesus Christ..."* (John 17:3; see also Phil. 3:10).

I encourage praying this daily for your own life and for the people around you. If you want God to be revealed to you, begin doing this today. Start by praying the following right now:

God, I pray that You would give me the Spirit of wisdom and revelation so that I may know You better. I pray that my eyes would be opened in order to know the hope to which You have called me. God, I ask that You would wake me up in areas that I am asleep or cannot see. I ask that You would reveal Yourself to me today. I ask that You would strengthen my spirit man to come alive and be vibrant so that I may see You, hear from You, and know You. In Jesus' name. Amen.

Chapter 5

WALKING IT OUT

The Word of God is the food, by which
prayer is nourished and made strong.
—E.M. BOUNDS, *The Necessity of Prayer*

"ARE YOU COMING to the prayer meeting tonight?" I was asked one Friday night, while still at the office. I made every excuse in the book why I couldn't make it to the prayer gathering that I had helped organize. "There are going to be about four hundred people," he said, as he continued trying to persuade me to attend. This was a really good-sized prayer meeting focused on interceding for the city. Emphatically, I responded with a big, "No, I have too much work to do."

While directing evangelistic campaigns with Impact World Tour, a ministry of Youth With A Mission (YWAM), I have facilitated many events around the world. Alongside the campaigns, I would set up citywide prayer gatherings sometimes on a weekly basis, where the city or region would pray and even fast for their area. I have seen many miracles as a direct result of these prayer gatherings. Even though I had seen so many great results, I personally had no real interest in attending or participating in a prayer meeting. I simply thought it was not "my thing." The agonizing wait until the meeting was done (they could last for an hour or sometimes two) was overwhelming for me. I merely found the whole process to be too hard and boring; and besides, I was not made for it. I told myself: I was a man of "action." I will do the work, and let those who pray support what I do or what I am part of.

I undeniably had it *all wrong,* as Hudson Taylor's words concur:

> But has the whole Church ever, since the days before
> Pentecost, ever put aside every other work and waited
> for Him for ten days, that power might be manifested?...
> We have given too much attention to methods, and to
> machinery, and resources, and too little to the Source
> of Power[1]

For far too long I gave all my attention to working and doing tasks in my own strength with very little power. Looking back now, I can see that other people were actually praying for the work that I was getting credit for.

After God showed me that real intimacy comes from spending time with Him and that true power to do the work comes from His Spirit, I had to find out how to live this lifestyle for myself. I didn't want to live it through anyone else. I didn't want to pretend to know God and talk about Him without actually *knowing Him*. I wanted the raw reality of God for myself.

I had so many questions. What do I do now? How do I do this? How do I pray? How do I do the exploits described in the Bible? How do I act upon all the things that I know I can partake of? How can I know God in a culture that is completely contrary to the things of the Spirit?

Unlocking these questions would prove to be simple. It was *prayer*. Having a prayer life and constantly seeking His face was the answer to all those questions. Prayer was never meant to be boring, merely done out of duty and only for results. Rather, it is in the place of encounter with God where our spirit is energized as we grow to love Him more. It positions us to be energized to love God and people by receiving God's love. Real power comes from spending time with Him and in knowing and communing with Him.

PRAYER

What *is* prayer? It is simply talking to God. It is a great privilege, a fierce struggle and a powerful miracle. Prayer is the best way out of a life of despair and the only way into the life of the overcomer.

Many people have this common question and I agree with Mike Bickle who said, "Why does God want us to pray? He wants us to connect with His heart in deep partnership. It is amazing that God pleads with us to pray, instead of us pleading with Him to listen."[2] People often wonder how to pray and what to pray. Many people take the time to pray and draw a blank and then come to the conclusion that it is just too hard. They either quit or pray powerless, defeated prayers.

POWER IN PRAYER AND THE WORD

Would you like your prayers to be more powerful? It begins by meditating and praying the Word of God. Hebrews 4:12 says: *"The word of God is alive and active* [powerful]. *Sharper than any double-edged sword..."* (NIV). When we speak and pray the Scriptures, we are coming into agreement with God, and His power is released to answer our prayers.

...He always [forever] *lives to make intercession for them* (Hebrews 7:25b).

The remarkable reality that Jesus lives forever interceding for me is tremendously encouraging and uplifting. The Father has deep and wonderful plans in His heart. He ordained that Jesus speak and verbalize them (intercession) as the way to release the Spirit's power as it was in creation. Father God had the plan to create, Jesus spoke it into existence, and the Holy Spirit created it. Jesus is the Creator who said, *"Let there be light"* in Genesis 1:3. The authority of our prayers when praying the Word is powerful and effective.

THE WORD

One of my favorite times in my married life occurred when my wife and I were lying in bed for the night after talking about the Word being *alive* and *active* (see Heb. 4:12). We said to each other, "Let's see how many Scripture verses we can say out loud to one another from memory before we fall asleep." It didn't matter what verses they were, or how short or long, we began saying them to each other. It was so much fun and it became a little competitive, which I personally enjoyed.

This went on for quite awhile, back and forth. I think I won by quoting more Scriptures—my wife may disagree. The point is, we woke up the following morning realizing that while we slept that night, we had Scriptures reverberating through our minds all night long! It felt like we were awake all night and we should have been tired and exhausted, but to our surprise we weren't. We woke up refreshed, with our spirits alive and vibrant! This was the first time that I had experienced the Word like this—so real and tangible, so alive! How fun it is to meditate on His Word *"day and night"* (see Josh. 1:8).

The most substantial way in which we can bolster our prayer lives is by *eating* the Word of God. This includes engaging in active conversation with God as we read His Word. Scripture gives us the best "conversational material" for our prayer life. Using this method makes prayer more enjoyable, and it goes deep into our spirit.

> *This Book of the Law shall not depart from your mouth, but you shall meditate in it day and night....then you will make your way prosperous, and then you will have good success* (Joshua 1:8).

Meditating on the Word of God is key for a prosperous life. Meditating is very simple. Here are things to remember: Take the Word and repeat it slowly. Think about it, speak it, ask the Holy Spirit about it; sing it and share about it. It's that simple. This process will renew your mind, transform your emotions, guide your life, and strengthen you!

Bible study must lead to dialogue with God. Jesus rebuked the Pharisees, saying:

> *You search the Scriptures, for in them you think you have...life; and these are they which testify of Me. But you are not willing to come to Me* [in dialogue] *that you may have life* (John 5:39-40).

We proactively take the words from the Bible and speak them back to God. The will of God for us is in His Word and the best way for circumstances in our lives to change is to make a commitment to pray His Word out loud every day.

Romans 10:17 says: *"So then faith comes by hearing, and hearing by the word of God."* It sounds so simple, but by doing this we are releasing power, because we are praying in victory. It is important to pray the prayers out loud, even if it is a whisper. The spoken Word makes things happen!

While praying, speaking, and meditating on the Word of God, I want to encourage you that the pursuit of the Word is the pursuit of the Person, Jesus, who is the Word of God.

> *Then the LORD said to me, "You have seen well, for I am ready to perform my Word"* (Jeremiah 1:12).

We actively commune with God about His Word. We also thank Him for particular truths that we read. We can even declare them. It is always important to ask God to reveal those truths to our lives. After all, it is the Holy Spirit who enlightens and illuminates the Word of God to our hearts (see Eph. 1:17-18). For example, pray:

> *Father, reveal to me the certainty of Your love, forgiveness, direction, and provision for me.*

STRENGTHEN YOUR PRAYER LIFE

> *Don't pray when you feel like it. Have an appointment with the Lord and keep it. A man is powerful on his knees.* —CORRIE TEN BOOM

Mike Bickle gives some insightful keys in his book, *Prayers to Strengthen Your Inner Man:*

> Begin by setting a schedule for regular prayer times. Then make a prayer list, and lastly have a right view of God. A schedule establishes "when" we will pray. A prayer list gives us focus on "what" to pray. And a right view of God causes us to "want" to pray.
>
> Most people will increase their prayer life dramatically by simply developing a schedule and prayer list. Many who love God never develop a consistent prayer life because they lack these disciplines. Here are some examples that will spur you on in your quest for a strong prayer life."[3]

PRAYER LISTS

The following prayer lists are adapted from Mike Bickle's teaching:

1. *"Prayer for our personal lives:* Breakthrough in our inner man (heart), circumstances (physical, financial, relational) and ministry that God's power may be released through our hands and words (singing/speaking) as we receive prophetic revelation to help others.

2. *Prayer for others (people and places):* Individuals, ministries, marketplace and governmental authorities, and the destiny of cities or nations.

3. *Prayer for others (strategic issues in society):* Government (elections, abortion), oppression (human trafficking), natural disasters (hurricane, drought), disease (AIDS, Avian bird flu), social crisis (famine, genocide, etc.) or economic crisis, etc."[4]

OTHER TOOLS

Another tool that I use to strengthen my prayer life includes journaling. Take time to record thoughts and prayers as you "pray-read" through Scripture. This helps us capture the truths that the Spirit gives us and to grow in our prayer dialogue with God. You can also write letters to and from God to encourage different forms of dialogue with Him.

FASTING

Yet another rewarding tool is *fasting*. Yes, you heard me correctly: *fasting*. Even though we will talk about fasting in greater length in a later chapter, I want to emphasize this as one of the most extraordinary tools that will thrust you to new levels in your spiritual walk. Fasting will propel you to break away from the status quo. While considering fasting as a lifestyle, or even doing a onetime shot of fasting, it may be regarded as *radical*, however, I believe the opposite to be true. God meant fasting to be a basic part of Christianity.

> *Moreover, when you fast, do not be like the hypocrites, with a sad countenance. For they disfigure their faces that they may appear to men to be fasting. Assuredly, I say to you, they have their reward. But you, when you fast, anoint your head and wash your face, so that you do not appear to men to be fasting, but to your Father who is in the secret place; and your Father who sees in secret will reward you openly* (Matthew 6:16-18).

What stands out about this particular passage is not only the instruction for fasting, but its references to *when* you fast. Fasting is meant to be a basic and fundamental part of Christianity that, when implemented in our lifestyle, is extremely powerful. Denying our physical man allows our spirit man to expand. Fasting is not only for the strong or the radicals; it is the greatest form of humility that positions our hearts to be dependent on God alone. Fasting is for everyone, in every sphere of society, the weak, the ordinary, and the strong. It is for every individual who desperately wants more of God. Fasting is an available tool to expand our spiritual capacity for more of Jesus!

All of these tools are available to us right *now*. All we have to do is ask the Lord for help and He helps us. So ask Him to help you and He is right there!

GOD'S GRACE

To walk this out on a daily basis we need God's grace. There will be days when we will have great success, and there will be other days when we will miss it. All He wants is for us to posture our hearts toward Him and start moving. Soon we will discover that we are growing stronger in Him. Regardless of where we are in our journey, we need an increase of God's grace on our lives and all we have to do is simply ask Him for it. I have a good friend who always reminds me, that God places His "super" on our "natural."

Chapter 6

LIFE WITH VISION

So teach us to number our days; that we
may gain a heart of wisdom. —Moses

DURING ONE OF Reverend Billy Graham's last television interviews he was asked, "If you were to do things over again, would you do things differently?"

Without any hesitation and full of emotion, Reverend Graham responded, "Yes, I would study more, pray more, travel less, take less speaking engagements. I took too many of them and too many places around the world. If I were to do it over again, I would spend more time in meditation and prayer and just telling the Lord how much I love Him and adore Him, and I'm looking forward to our time we are going to spend together for eternity."[1]

This is such a compelling response. At the end of such an incredible career and life, if Billy Graham could do things differently, he would spend more time in prayer, telling the Lord how much He loves Him and adores Him. He would meditate on the Word and take fewer speaking engagements, if he could do it over again. Wow!

Would that be our reply? Do we look back at the time here on earth with the same perspective of wishing we had spent more time with God, studying His Word, speaking to Him in prayer, and getting to know the Creator of the universe?

I would challenge us to take heed to these important thoughts of how we spend our time here on earth. Billy Graham lived a life that most people would only have dreamt about, speaking to millions, building a large organization, connecting with the highest-profile figures of his time—and Billy Graham answers by saying that he would have spent more time with God. Let's learn from this great man's wisdom and personal experience.

REDEEMING TIME

See then that you walk circumspectly, not as fools but as wise, redeeming the time, because the days are evil (Ephesians 5:15-16).

Scripture makes it clear that time is valuable in our relationship with God. Therefore, how we spend our time is an important part of our lives. Without an intentional, organized approach to time management, the gift of time can be easily squandered, leaving us with regret and a lack of fruit in our lives.

JONATHAN EDWARDS' RESOLUTIONS

Let me provoke you to contemplation and action by showing you the resolution of a person I consider one of the greatest men in history, Jonathan Edwards.

One of the most eminent American philosophers and theologians of his time, Jonathan Edwards became the first president of Princeton University. Edwards was one of the key figures in the First Great Awakening in the

1730s. Edwards spent the majority of his life as a preacher, theologian, and missionary affecting countless lives.[2]

Abundant fruit was evident in his devoted-to-God life. The following are some of Edwards' resolutions concerning time, from the book, *The Unwavering Resolve of Jonathan Edwards*:

> Resolved, never to lose one moment of time, but to improve it in the most profitable way I possibly can.[3]

> Resolved, to live with all my might, while I do live.[4]

> Resolved, never to do anything, which I should be afraid to do, if it were the last hour of my life.[5]

Billy Graham and Jonathan Edwards both showed how much they valued time. This is one of the main things they thought about in their pursuit of God. We should too.

There is a great war in our lives that affects the workplace, schools, and churches, etc. The battle is between diligence and slothfulness. I show you these to encourage you that diligence has a great reward.

DILIGENCE AND SLOTH

Paul exhorted the saints to use the spiritual gifts, such as prophecy, teaching, leadership, and giving. (Rom. 12:6-8). When Paul mentioned leadership, he emphasized those who lead should do so "with diligence" (Rom. 12:8). Although diligence is not the only leadership issue, it is a critical component of leadership and is the most commonly neglected. Diligence in leadership is a rare but very valuable quality.

Diligence, as defined by one dictionary, is "the constant and earnest effort to accomplish what is undertaken with persistent exertion." We must recognize that leadership is not halfhearted, but is earnest in its efforts. It is not by definition something that is done on a short-term basis. A diligent leader is one who takes initiative in a long-term way. It lasts for more than one summer or one semester of school, or even one year....

Some people have skill because of natural gifting, but they lack in using their God-given skills. Thus, they will never reach the fullness of God's plan for their life. Solomon wisely stated, "He who has a slack hand becomes poor, but the hand of the diligent makes rich" (Prov. 10:4).[6]

Slothfulness is not innocent, but sinful and destructive as it squanders one's inheritance from God. The Church in the Western culture with its false message of grace exalts slothfulness and regards diligence as legalism, unless it is in pursuit of pleasure.

We must never apologize for our insistence on diligence. Measure the fruit of the diligent compared to the slothful. Who would you rather imitate? In order to bear the fruit of the diligent, we must understand some of our life-given resources. I would like to show you the direction and vision on how to get there. So let's examine the resources God has given us.

LIFE RESOURCES

God has given us some incredible life resources. It has been said that money is power. Money *is* very powerful; it can make a great impact. People take risks in finances all of the time, sometimes making more money and other times losing it all. Some spend their money on things that don't really matter. Regardless of your view on finances, if you are a good steward and if you are an extravagant giver, you can always get more.

To squander time however, is to waste life. It is to squander destiny. Aimless people in the realm of time, squander time. To squander hours may not seem like much of an impact to many people, but when we throw away hours and minutes, we really squander our destiny.

Here is a list of God-given life resources. As you look at this list and consider each area, determine whether you are investing in it or squandering it. There is one thing for sure: we shouldn't waste these valuable life resources.

Life Resources Include:

1. Your time

2. Your affection

3. Your money

4. Your talents

Each of these life resources is so vital for a vibrant, balanced life. Living with regret is one of the worst things to face during our time here on earth. Let's make the most of our life resources. I would like to help you build and strengthen any new resolutions concerning time. It begins with vision.

VISION FOR LIFE

"Where there is no vision, the people are unrestrained..." declares Solomon in Proverbs 29:18 (NASB). In other words, without a clear purpose for our lives, we will most likely become distracted and live without necessary restraints. It is interesting how many of the people on Earth plan their lives, especially in Western cultures. There is planning for our future finances, education, jobs, children, etc. But in all of this, Christians rarely have a plan for their life in God.

Developing an overall life vision is the plumb line, or the measuring stick of your activity and time management. It is the first step in ensuring that we love God in a manner that reflects the first commandment and causes the second commandment to flow from it on a personal and consistent basis.

> *Jesus said to him, "You shall love the LORD your God with all your heart, with all your soul, and with all your mind. This is the first and great commandment. And the second is like it: 'You shall love your neighbor as yourself'"* (Matthew 22:37-39).
>
> Loving God is the first priority. Jesus did not call it the first option, but a commandment. Jesus makes it clear that cultivating love for Him is the first emphasis of the Holy Spirit. Loving God is a glorious end in itself; however, it never ends with loving God but always overflows with loving ourselves and others (believers and unbelievers).[7]

There is no other starting place for our life vision than the place of loving God. God chose the human response to be the channel in which we express love. How we love God is expressed in how we live our lives and how we live our lives should be guided by our life vision.

We should seek to have long-term goals (over the next ten years) and short-term goals (over three months to three years) in each area of our lives. This is a proven way to maximize fruitfulness in our lives. There are several areas to consider when setting goals. Our spiritual life, relationships, work life, ministry, finances, health, and leisure activities are all important spheres of our lives that call for clear goals and time allotments.

As I said before, we should not live with regret. As you take time to set goals and establish them in your life's routine, everything you do will become a reality instead of a pipe dream.

Proverbs 29:18 says you will *"perish"* (KJV) or *"cast off restraint"* (NIV) if you have no vision. To perish means you will waste your life, and squander your inheritance. You will not fulfill your destiny. If you don't have your vision clearly written, you will never know what you're aiming for.

The following are a few vision statements that I have personally made, along with my wife, for one another and also for our children. They describe what type of home and lifestyle we aspire to have. In no way am I declaring that I have reached this; I haven't, but this is what my wife and I desire to be said about us at the end of our lives. You may want to use these as examples to help you aim for something greater in your life.

LIFE VISIONS

As an Individual

I unashamedly desire to be an extravagant lover of God whom God knows and whom God calls, "a man after My heart." I resolve to be a lifelong student of the Word of God and a great deliverer of men. I desire to lead as many people as possible to God's heart and face, with all of my strength.

As a Couple

We wholeheartedly resolve to live our lives in light of eternity; to build treasures in heaven where moth and rust do not destroy. We determine to live our lives knowing our days are few and the days are evil. We resolve to walk face to face in love, unity, and partnership; to fulfill all that God has for us.

As a Husband

> *Husbands, love your wives, just as Christ loved the church and gave Himself for her...* (Ephesians 5:25).

75

I resolve to be a husband who extravagantly loves his wife and serves her as Christ serves the Church and gave His life for her. I determine to live my life fully devoted in love with Christelle.

As a Wife

> *Who can find a virtuous wife? For her worth is far above rubies* (Proverbs 31:10).

I resolve to be a woman who loves deeply through respect and building a home for Antonio that is a refuge. I determine to have a relationship with true intimacy, to be a helpmate to him in all things, to think of him above myself, and to bring him good all of my days.

For Our Children

> *Behold, children are a heritage from the* LORD, *the fruit of the womb is a reward. Like arrows in the hand of a warrior, so are the children of one's youth* (Psalm 127:3-4).

Our greatest aspiration is to have godly children who know their God and His heart through His Word and daily communion. We determine to raise them as kings and priests before their God. They will be raised in a home that is God-centered and is countercultural. They will be trained to do great exploits and reach higher levels in God than we ever do. They will be set apart unto God, to be voices in their generation.

Our children will see the love between us. They will view first-hand our victories and failures. But most of all, they will have living examples of obedience to God, to see our lives as "yes" to God. We will shape their minds and mold their lives to make waves upon the shores of nations. Our children will fear God and marry spouses who fear God and they will raise a lineage that fears the Lord, and we will practically equip them to do so.

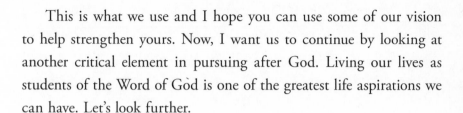

This is what we use and I hope you can use some of our vision to help strengthen yours. Now, I want us to continue by looking at another critical element in pursuing after God. Living our lives as students of the Word of God is one of the greatest life aspirations we can have. Let's look further.

KNOWING THE WORD OF GOD

This Book of the Law shall not depart from your mouth, but you shall meditate in it day and night, that you may observe to do according to all that is written in it. For then you will make your way prosperous, and then you will have good success (Joshua 1:8).

Most people, full of sincerity, think they read the Bible, the Word of God—but they really don't. The plan of God is that we encounter the Man, Jesus, through the written Word.

The fruit of a person who is not walking in the Word of God is always obvious. Today's anointing is no guarantee that you will have it five years from now. It really doesn't matter if you had training or that you walked in a certain anointing in the past; you can lose it if you don't daily maintain a life in the Word. The life of God is released through the Word that will transform every aspect of your life.

The Word of God builds you up. A powerful New Testament reality is that we have the mind of Christ. Knowing the Word will give you an inheritance among believers. We have an inheritance in this life. If you are too busy to get into the Word of God, you are too busy to get your inheritance. Your inheritance has conditions to enter into the fullness of God. They are related to the Word of God in your life. Knowing the Word of God for yourself has to be a part of your life vision.

VISION

Earlier I shared with you a portion of my own life vision, along with my family's. I have also touched on the vital inheritance that we get from being students of the Word of God on a daily basis. I encourage you to make your own life vision and if you have a family, create it together with your spouse.

When beginning the process of creating your life vision, you are identifying your core values and then developing the language to communicate them from a heart level that is clear and helpful. Try to avoid too much "fluffy" wording. Write your intentions clearly and even hang the statement on a wall in your home or at work.

When creating a vision statement, it should describe what you would like to be known for at the end of your life. Take time in making this vision, and allow the Lord to stir your heart with the reality of your time here on Earth. During this process, I have seen many people align themselves with what they really desire and hope for. This is a great exercise.

GOALS

The next step in fulfilling your vision is to make some goals. The likelihood of your achieving your life vision without setting goals to guide you in obtaining the vision is very slim. Zig Ziglar explains, "Studies show that less than 3 percent of Americans set goals."[8] The vast majority of that small percentage are the wealthiest in the nation.

Mainly, people do not lack the time, or the energy to begin to achieve their life vision. They *lack direction*. Goal-setting gives us that direction needed to ensure that we are going for our life vision. George T. Doran has created a S.M.A.R.T. system and I have found it to work very well. When thinking about goals, if you use this it will increase your ability to not only achieve the goals of your life and your life vision, but it will assist you tremendously in your action plan.

S.M.A.R.T is an acronym, which I have used in a slightly different way from Doran's online list:

- **Specific:** Make your goals detailed, clear, and well thought out.

- **Measureable:** It is beneficial to have short-term measurements built into your goals. Though this will fall into your action plan, begin to think in these terms while creating your goals.

- **Attainable:** Identify goals that are most important to you, and then begin to discover the attitudes, abilities, skills, and financial capabilities to facilitate attaining them.

- **Relevant:** Relevant means setting goals that ensure the actions fit into your overall life vision. It is unrealistic to set a goal that has no basis in your vocation, ministry, or life vision.

- **Time-bound:** We must set time frames to our goals. Are they next month? Next semester? Next decade?[9]

Let's continue; I want to begin to help you by asking a question. *What are your life goals?* Your goals should be set in seven specific areas:

1. Spiritual Life (prayer time, fasting, Bible study, etc.)

2. Relationships (family, friends, etc.)

3. Work (marketplace calling, etc.)

4. Ministry (in the Church, outside the Church, etc.)

5. Finances (spending, giving, saving, investing, etc.)

6. Health (exercise, diet, etc.)

7.   Leisure Activity (recreation, vacation, play, enter-
     tainment, sports, etc.)

Apply your life vision to these seven specific areas of your life.
Write out your short-term goals (three months to three years) and
long-term goals (over ten years) for each area. A helpful hint in making your life goals would be to come from a position of *reaching for
the light* not *running from darkness.*

Once goals have been set for our lives, we must not lose focus,
or some goals may become unattainable. It is one thing to have goals
articulated on paper and another thing to be living them out. For
some people, when goals are written, it seems intimidating to actually "walk them out." That is why keeping a schedule is helpful.
One effective way to stay on task with our goals is by making an
action plan.

ACTION PLAN

I want to encourage you to make an action plan. Describe your
strategy to accomplish both your short-term and long-term goals.
What will you actually *do* to make these life goals become a reality?
Determine the course of action that you will take to make each one
of these short-term and long-term goals happen.

Let me help by explaining further. Let's say that you would
like to study the Book of Ephesians. That is a great spiritual goal.
The following example demonstrates how to implement this in
your life:

1.   Spiritual Goal: To study the Book of Ephesians

2.   Objectives:

     a. To understand the Ephesian Church and apply
         this understanding to my life.

b. To be able to clearly communicate its main themes and message.

c. To understand the overall framework of the book.

d. To comprehensively understand God through this book.

e. To dialogue with the Holy Spirit about the verses in Ephesians and allow Him to speak to me and make it alive in my heart.

Writing down your action plan and objectives effectively helps you fulfill your goals and your overall life vision. But there is one major thing that everything hinges upon: a schedule.

SCHEDULE

The most vital part is creating a schedule. A schedule helps us to increase our focus and our level of actually attaining our vision and goals, by putting our plans into action. Without a daily schedule it is easy to lose focus and needlessly waste time. This is where the rubber meets the road. Without a schedule and and a commitment to maintain it, even the sincerest vision will go unfulfilled.

We must learn how to commit to our varying projects within the hours available each week. This is where the majority of us get derailed: we fail to focus our lives in order to accomplish our vision.

To start, I recommend that you take the 168 hours contained in each week and start scheduling everything from sleep, eating, prayer times, family time, work time, entertainment, etc., by breaking down whole sections of the week into one-hour increments.

SUMMARY

John Wesley said, "I have so much to do that I spend several hours in prayer before I am able to do it."[10]

Living a busy lifestyle *and* spending time with the Lord can be challenging. The challenge is not insurmountable however. It is a matter of establishing the priority and making it the number one focus.

Simply put, the question is this: What is our focus, and what are our priorities, first and foremost? When we want something badly enough, we find a way to align our lives to accommodate it. Priority and desire are connected. Let's put some legs to our God-given desires and use our resources wisely.

Chapter 7

KEYS TO INTIMACY

Spell this out in capital letters: THE HOLY
SPIRIT IS A PERSON. He is not enthusiasm.
He is not courage. He is not energy. He is not the
personification of all good qualities, like Jack Frost
is the personification of cold weather. Actually,
the Holy Spirit is not the personification of
anything....He has individuality. He is one being
and not another. He has will and intelligence. He
has hearing. He has knowledge and sympathy and
ability to love and see and think. He can hear,
speak, desire, grieve and rejoice. He is a Person.
—A. W. TOZER, "The 'Person' of the Holy Spirit"

SOME TIME AGO, Christelle and I called our two older boys,
Michael and Gabriel, into the living room on a summer day. We
gave them a short teaching from the Bible on the person of the Holy
Spirit: who He is, that He speaks to us, and that we can hear from
Him. We went further and told them that we can speak to Him and

that He hears us. We shared with them that He is God and what He says is true. Anytime He comes into the room, He brings joy and peace. He may bring to light sin in our lives. But with repentance, He brings forgiveness and removes shame. We told them about His presence. There is nothing like being in His manifest presence.

After about a twenty-minute discussion, I told them that we were going to talk to Him right now and we were going to listen to Him. He was going to speak to us and we were going to share what He said. I turned on some worship music in the background. I said to my boys, "We will be still in His presence and then when you want to, I want you to ask the Holy Spirit one question, 'God, what do You think about me?' I don't want you to say anything else, just wait on Him. Wait until He says something."

Then I invited the Holy Spirit to increase His presence among us. We all closed our eyes and just sat still in His presence. I would open my eyes once in a while just to see if they were following my instructions. I noticed that their postures became soft and relaxed. Our second son, Gabriel, had tears streaming down his cheeks, with his eyes closed in God's presence. I could sense the sweet presence of God all over and around us. It was such a tender time in His presence.

After about fifteen minutes, I asked Michael, who is introspective and wise, if God said anything to him. With watery eyes, he said, "Yes, God told me that *He loves me.*"

I enjoyed listening to Michael say this, because we can't get enough of hearing how much God likes us and loves us. I then turned to Gabriel, who is tender and compassionate, and asked him what God said. His response really surprised me, "God said I was *cool on the inside and cool on the outside.*"

The Holy Spirit is a person and knows just what to say to each one of us—He's awesome! Years later, these simple words have been monumental in building the boys' confidence with the Lord.

That day we introduced the person *Holy Spirit* to our kids. Or a better way to put it, we gave language to what they have probably already felt, heard, and saw. Since that day we have continued to give God room to speak to us as a family and to each of our family members. The Holy Spirit brings life, comfort, joy, peace, freedom, direction, and so many other things that we need; but more than that, we have communion with God through the person of the Holy Spirit.

Having an understanding of who the Holy Spirit is, and who He is not, is critical in order to experience His presence and power. The Holy Spirit is not a feeling or an emotion, although His presence can stir up emotions within you. He is the third person of the Trinity. When you receive Jesus Christ as your Lord and Savior, the Holy Spirit comes to live within you; you become His dwelling place. As you learn to yield to Him, you will find yourself walking out God's plan for your life in greater and greater ways. In addition, you will experience supernatural power and breakthrough like never before.

Jesus explains the function of the Holy Spirit in John 16:7:

> *Nevertheless I tell you the truth. It is to your advantage that I go away; for if I do not go away, the Helper will not come to you; but if I depart, I will send Him to you.*

Jesus knew He would have to leave in order for the Holy Spirit to come to the earth. Now that the Holy Spirit is here, and dwelling in us, the power of God can flow to an even greater extent than when Jesus walked the earth!

Since we are living in the Last Days, it is going to be imperative that you know how to distinguish the Holy Spirit's voice. The feeling that we sometimes describe as intuition or a hunch is often the Holy Spirit. You can develop discernment of His voice through studying and meditating on the Word of God and spending time with

Him. He will never say anything to you that doesn't line up with the written Word; therefore, studying the Bible is essential to your recognizing His voice.

THE PERSON—HOLY SPIRIT

Each of our five children is known for different things. The contrasts in personality and character are well known to their siblings and friends. For example, our third son, Elijah, is fiery and passionate in everything he does. Our little girl Isabella is tenderhearted, forgives easily, and is generous.

In the same way, the Holy Spirit is known by certain characteristics and roles. The following are some biblical roles of the Holy Spirit:

He Speaks

> He who has an ear let him hear what the Spirit says to the churches. To him who overcomes, I will give to eat from the tree of life, which is in the midst of the Paradise of God (Revelation 2:7).

> As they ministered to the Lord and fasted, the Holy Spirit said, "Now separate to Me Barnabas and Saul for the work to which I have called them" (Acts 13:2).

He Intercedes

> In the same way the Spirit also helps our weakness; for we do not know how to pray as we should, but the Spirit Himself intercedes for us with groanings too deep for words. (Romans 8:26 NASB).

He Leads

> Then the Spirit said to Philip, "Go near and overtake this chariot" (Acts 8:29).

For as many as are led by the Spirit of God, these are sons of God (Romans 8:14).

He Commands

Now when they had gone through Phrygia and the region of Galatia, they were forbidden by the Holy Spirit to preach the word in Asia. After they had come to Mysia, they tried to go into Bithynia, but the Spirit did not permit them (Acts 16:6-7).

He Guides

However, when He, the Spirit of truth, has come, He will guide you into all truth; for He will not speak on His own authority, but whatever He hears He will speak; and He will tell you things to come (John 16:13).

He Can Be Insulted

Of how much worse punishment, do you suppose, will he be thought worthy who has trampled the Son of God underfoot, counted the blood of the covenant by which he was sanctified a common thing, and insulted the Spirit of grace? (Hebrews 10:29).

He Can Be Grieved

And do not grieve the Holy Spirit of God, by whom you were sealed for the day of redemption (Ephesians 4:30).

Communion

When you acknowledge the Holy Spirit and commune with Him on a daily basis, He will show you mysteries and the secret plans of God for your life. Jeremiah 33:3 says: *"Call to Me, and I will answer you, and show you great and mighty things, which you do not know."*

He will guide you into your destiny when you allow Him to direct your decisions. When you call on the Holy Spirit, you may say, "Holy Spirit, I don't know what to do in this situation, but I know You know the answer. Show me what to do."

You can cultivate your relationship with the Holy Spirit by praising God, praying, and singing spiritual songs (see Eph. 5:19). Doing these things helps to build your spirit and makes you more sensitive to His presence. Invite Him into every situation and atmosphere in which you find yourself. When you acknowledge Him this way, He will be able to move in your life.

Since the Holy Spirit was sent to help guide and direct your life, it is important that you set aside time every day to fellowship with Him. Talk with Him as you would a close friend or family member. Let Him know your concerns and talk to Him about the Bible. He will give you the revelation, insight, and enlightenment you need to lead you into the good life God has prepared for you.

Developing a relationship with the Holy Spirit is going to cost you something. It will mean getting up to pray when you don't feel like it and letting go of old habits and mindsets that oppose God's Word. But when you create an environment in which the Holy Spirit can dwell, the rich rewards you will reap in your relationship with Him will far outweigh anything else.

Keys To Intimacy

Intimacy is of the utmost importance in responding to God's pursuit. Having an understanding of how to develop an intimate walk with the person Holy Spirit is crucial for a long and strong relationship with God. Here are some important keys to growing in intimacy, and some things that will stop your growth as well. It's important that we understand both the things that will help us grow and things that will hinder and stunt our growth with the Lord.

Humility

>...*God resists the proud, but gives grace to the humble*
>(1 Peter 5:5).

I agree with John Bevere in his book, *Drawing Near*, on the importance of humility.[1] I would include my own thoughts. Have you ever been with a person who is humble? Humility is one of the most attractive traits any person can have. I have been with charismatic people and those who make others laugh. They are fun people and I end up having a good time with them. But those with great humility and meekness, are very attractive, no matter what their appearance. Humility is one of the most important keys to intimacy with God.

God is drawing us close to His heart. He is passionately pursuing us. Humility is the drawing card. Without humility we won't even get close. Humility is the single greatest agent that allows the Lord to move in our lives. Humility is the opposite of pride. When we live in pride, God cannot stand to be in our presence. It is the complete opposite of who He is and what He represents. When we walk in humility, God will release the grace that we need. I can't say it enough: humility is our greatest key to intimacy with God. Great men throughout the Bible understood this: David, Joseph, Peter, Paul, and Moses.

>*Now the man Moses was very humble, more than all men*
>*who were on the face of the earth.* (Numbers 12:3).

This statement is unparalleled: *He is the most humble man on the face of the earth.* Could you imagine saying this about someone? The question is, who wrote the Book of Numbers? Moses did! Now this is startling. Moses wasn't being arrogant; he was simply stating a fact. Because all Scripture is Spirit-breathed, Moses knew it to be true.

Humility is one of the greatest keys to intimacy with God. Moses spoke to God face to face as a man speaks to a friend (see Exod. 33:11).

Living in humility enables you to breathe the very air that God breathes. It is the essence of entering into His presence. You know when you're walking in His presence because you will look and act with great humility. In fact, the greater the humility in your life, the greater intimacy you will have with God.

HUNGER

John G. Lake described the starved spirit:

> Now, if your spirit has reached the place where it has no appetite for the things of God, you have been playing hooky. You have been feeding on things you ought not eat and you have compelled your poor spirit to feed on trash and cheap scandal and cheap talk and useless talk, wise cracking and everything, and you have never given your spirit any real healthy food for a long time, and the poor thing is dying of hunger.[2]

Hunger is a great persuader. It is a powerful motivator. Nations have learned that you can do most anything with people if they are hungry. But when they are hungry you also want to watch out. There is a certain spirit of desperation that accompanies hunger. The same is true of spiritual hunger. I can guarantee you that after the crucifixion of Jesus there were a hundred and twenty *very* spiritually hungry men and women in Jerusalem in the upper room as described in Acts. I do not believe, if they had not been extremely hungry and expectant, that they would have gotten so powerfully filled. It was *because* of this that the Holy Spirit filled them. There are countless other stories of men and woman who hungered after the Lord and He met them. There were those who hungered desperately and what followed was a move of God that birthed Christianity today.

Blessed are those who hunger and thirst for righteousness,
for they shall be filled (Matthew 5:6).

God's purposes come to pass when our hearts and minds have a real "God cry," a real "God prayer" comes into our spirit, and a real "God thirst" gets in our nature. Something is going to happen. If this becomes the supreme cry of your heart, He will meet you. Crying out for God can't be second, third, or fourth. It must be the number one issue. If all the powers and energies of your spirit, soul, and your whole body are reaching out and crying to God, He will fill you.

Let me tell you, the last thing you want to leave for last is Jesus! The last thing you can afford to lose is hunger and passion after Him and His Word. You can't give, lead, or minister from emptiness and a dry heart. If we spend more time reading about God than cultivating a relationship with Him, something is wrong. Let's get hungry!

No matter what you do, or who you are, you can succeed in the regular work and mundane things of life with a heart *set* on the Lord. I would encourage you to take this time and ask Him to give you hunger; to allow you to be desperate for Him. The hunger *to hunger* is the first step. Begin crying out to Him. He will fill you and give you the desires of your heart!

Guarding Our Lips

Some keys to intimacy naturally function from the offensive stance. They are things that we must be proactive about and move forward in. Then there are other areas in which we play a defensive role. These are things that we resist, watch over, and keep a guard on. We take measures of defense to those things that are important to us.

Do not let any unwholesome talk come out of your mouths,
but only what is helpful for building others up according
to their needs, that it may benefit those who listen (Ephesians 4:29 NIV).

I will expand on this further in another chapter, but let's talk for a moment on the power of our speech. God wants to burn in and through us, but He simply cannot do that if our lips are not in line with Him and His Word. To stop speaking negatively is very important, but there are greater levels of being alert in our speech.

We need to allow the Holy Spirit to be comfortable in our presence. Imagine that. We must be constantly watchful and alert to the words that are coming out of our mouths so that the Holy Spirit can be comfortable with us and move in great power. I would suggest that one way we can begin to honor the Holy Spirit is by being attentive to our words.

OBEDIENCE AND DISOBEDIENCE

These words by Bill Johnson highlight the critical boundaries that are set in Scripture for hosting God's presence in our lives:

> We steward the presence of God by learning to obey the commands of God "Do not grieve the Holy Spirit" (Ephesians 4:30) and "Do not quench the Spirit" (1 Thessalonians 5:19). We grieve Him when we do something wrong; we quench Him when we fail to do what is right, stopping the flow of His love and power that comes from the Father.[3]

This means we don't ignore and cast away the commands of God. With the intention to obey Him fully, you set your heart to say "yes." Deliberate disobedience quenches the Holy Spirit. Remember, He is the only One who can reveal Jesus to you. If the Holy Spirit is quenched and grieved, you will not receive revelation of Jesus. You can't offend the Holy Spirit and drive Him away, and still expect Him to make Jesus known to your heart in a greater way.

REBELLION VERSUS IMMATURITY

Most of us are immature spiritually, but that is not at all the same as being rebellious. Nor is it the same as raising your fist toward heaven, saying, "No! I'm not obeying in this area. I want to do my will, and I don't care if it's wrong. I'm doing it anyway!"

You can ask for Spirit-revelation of God all you want to, but if you're deliberately disobedient, prayer will get you nowhere. Prayer is no substitute for the intention to obey. If you want to know Jesus intimately, you must receive the Word of God in your heart without purposefully resisting the Holy Spirit.

Are there areas of deliberate disobedience in your life? Maybe you are in a wrong relationship God cannot honor. Maybe it's a shady business deal. Maybe it's bitterness you won't let go of because someone has offended you and you want to get even. You keep slandering and putting down the person, every time his or her name is mentioned.

Resolve to be consistent and to confess and resist sin. Realize that God looks more at the sincerity of your motives to obey than at your actual attainment of spiritual maturity. Remember: one deliberate sin persisted in is fatal to the spiritual growth of the soul. Deliberate sin blocks spiritual progress and hinders your walk with the Lord. There's no substitute for a life set on obedience.

HIS PRESENCE

It is paramount to conclude this chapter by speaking about one of my favorite subjects: His presence. Let me share with you the first time I encountered His manifest presence in my life.

One Sunday night in 1990 when I was thirteen years old, I went to my home church in Minneapolis, Minnesota. I heard that Mylon Lefevre, a Christian music artist was going to be speaking at the service that night. I was really excited! I had been to his concerts before, but now I was going to get to see him in a more private setting.

My best friend, Adam, and I arrived early and sat near the front of the auditorium. We wanted to be as close as possible. Unbeknownst to us, Mylon Lefevre sat right in front of us. I can still see the cufflinks on his wrists: "M.F.," big and bold as he lifted his hands in worship. I thought they were so cool.

After he sang and spoke, I ran to foyer of the church to buy his newest CD. God used this CD to give me a taste of His presence. This left such an imprint on my spirit that it sealed for me the reality of His presence forever. I have tasted many earthly pleasures. I know the counterfeits and replicas. God's presence is beyond words. No high, no sensation, *nothing* compares to the sweet presence of the Holy Spirit.

I went home from church with my new CD. It was *Mylon's Greatest Hits*. My brother slept at a friend's house that night, so I had the room to myself. I couldn't wait to go to bed and put on the CD and relish each word from the songs. As I went through the whole CD, there was one song that really captured my attention. It was called, "More" (of Jesus). I put the song on repeat and let it play over and over again. I began to sing it from my heart to Him. I began to ask for more of Jesus in my life.

I knelt next to my bed, singing the song to my beloved Jesus. I began to speak to the Holy Spirit for the very first time. His presence became so real to me that from that point on in my life, I could sense if He was in the room.

There is such a sweet peace and joy when He enters my reality. Even if He is bringing conviction, rebuke, or discipline, He comes with overwhelming love and affection. I spent hours speaking to Him that night. I began to tell Him of my love for Him. My face was full of tears and my heart was full of indescribable emotion toward this person, Holy Spirit. I was fascinated by Him—the Creator of the universe. I was drawn to Jesus more than ever before in my life. The hunger and thirst that this moment gave me left me hungry for more.

We have talked about *His presence* throughout this book and highlighted it in various chapters; but there is something so awesome, contagious, and enticing about His presence. In His presence, nothing else matters, I don't care who you are. It doesn't matter where you are; when His presence is there, you know it. When God Almighty shows Himself, and you yield to His presence, there is nothing or no one that compares.

> *In Your presence is fullness of joy; at Your right hand are pleasures forevermore* (Psalm 16:11).

This is one of my favorite verses because God is the author of pleasure! He loves pleasure; it is the devil that has warped, twisted, and counterfeited what God intended for our enjoyment. Let's drink of His real, satisfying pleasure, and as the woman at the well was told by Jesus, *"whoever drinks of the water that I shall give him will never thirst"* (John 4:14a).

His presence brings fullness of joy. I love being in His presence for this very reason. I receive great joy and peace and I can't get enough of it. In His presence are pleasures forever and ever and ever. That is one of the reasons I believe angels just stand in awe in His presence: because it's so glorious and full of joy. Why would you want to go anywhere else?

God is preparing the Church of today for an outpouring of His Spirit on all flesh. He is getting the Church ready to walk in the supernatural. The Book of Acts is only a glimpse of the things to come. As He prepares us, He is filling us with His oil of intimacy and giving us amazing, desperate, and unfathomable hunger for Him and the things of God.

Chapter 8

PURSUIT OF HOLINESS

A baptism of holiness, a demonstration of
godly living is the crying need of our day.
—DUNCAN CAMPBELL

I N THE CYPRESS Hills of Southern Alberta, with our ministry team
at our annual staff retreat, I was struck with a statement that kept
running through my mind during our time of worship: *Humility is*
the on-ramp to holiness. I realized how much I need humility in order
to walk in holiness. I had never heard of this before, but it's actually unfathomable to walk in holiness without humility. To posture
ourselves in humility is the fastest way to encounter God. Humility
is our saying, "God I need you. I can't do this on my own." This
posture of our heart enables us to receive the fullness of God. In
essence, the greater the humility in our lives, the greater we are available for encounter.

Ultimately it's pride that justifies sin and it's pride that keeps us
from looking at our own hearts and the motivations of our hearts. I
couldn't agree more with Francis Frangipane's insightful truths that

"...holiness is the product of grace, and God gives grace to the humble."[1] In our desire to know God, we must understand what God is looking for: He resists the proud, but gives grace to the humble (see James 4:6). "Humility brings grace to our need, and grace alone can change our hearts."[2] Francis also unveils two main truths that God has led him to seek: "to know the heart of God in Christ and to know my own heart in Christ's light."[3] I would add that only the humble of heart will even dare look.

PURSUIT OF HOLINESS

We are in pursuit of holiness because the pursuit of holiness is the pursuit of God Himself. He is holy and He calls us to be holy and to be with Him. There is no separation of the pursuit of God and the pursuit of holiness. Holiness and God are synonymous. The pursuit of holiness requires us to come into agreement with Him. He is holy. He is pure. He is the very essence of holiness. "We are seeking the living God, for true holiness does not come from following rules; it comes from following Christ."[4]

> ...*without* [holiness], *no one will see the Lord* (Hebrews 12:14).

The very nature of man longs to see God and to know Him. Ever since I was a little boy, I wanted to see Him. I didn't want people to tell me what He looked like; I wanted to see Him for myself. I have read what Jesus physically looks like today (see Rev. 1). I also know that I can learn what He looks like by meditating on His character and attributes: how He loves, how He responds, how He is so giving, how He is slow to anger and abounding in love. He is love Himself. He is the very nature of love.

We all have a yearning to see Him. I pray that as you read this chapter, a desire to remove anything that hinders your ability to love and to see the one and only Jesus would come alive in you. I don't want to speak about rules and regulations. Those alone won't get you very far in the pursuit of holiness.

> The greatest revival and the greatest pressure in history will come in the generation in which Jesus returns. The light will increase at the same time that darkness increases. The wheat and the tares will mature together at the end of the age (see Matt. 13:30). Light will get brighter and darkness will get darker. Darkness is increasing and so is great light. Both are increasing at the same time.[5]

He is drawing His Church to His face and to His heart. The end-time Church will be victorious and full of God's glory. The Church will live in purity, without spot (compromise) or wrinkle. I believe God is getting ready to release more of His glory and more of His Spirit, but He desires a Church that will stand for truth and live in pursuit of holiness.

THE HALLWAY OF CURIOSITY

Walking down my junior high school hallway, putting away my books in my locker—it was a day that I will never forget. Totally unexpectedly and unaware came a temptation that eventually took my life into a dungeon of secret thoughts, emotions, and actions.

My buddy said to me, "Hey man, do you have any money?" I said, "For what?" "My brother gave me a *Playboy* magazine and I am selling each page for ten cents. It's only a dime."

Immediately my heart began to pound, knowing it was wrong to have this in my possession. "What would my parents think? How am I going to get this home? What's the point of looking at a naked body anyway?"

My curiosity burned inside of me. I wanted to look. I wanted to see what the big deal was all about. At the age of twelve, just entering seventh grade, I was only really interested in basketball, and nothing else. But I was intrigued, so I gave my buddy a dime. I didn't even look. I was so scared. I put it in my front pocket and it felt like I had fire in my jeans. I didn't know that it really was!

I went home and looked at pornography for the very first time. After a first glance, I folded it and hid it under a rug. I knew it was wrong. This started a fire that has taken years of learning, studying, confessing, fighting, releasing, receiving, and walking in step with the Spirit to obtain freedom and true joy.

I lived with years of shame over a habit that I desperately desired to be set free from. Even though I see and hear how many young men and women fall into the enemy's trap of immorality, I was not expecting it to happen to me.

In the beginning we justify it in our minds, being ignorant or oblivious of the effects of this sin, but at some point a person knows it's wrong and has to make a decision about what he or she really wants. "Purity begins with our determined refusal to hide from the condition of our hearts."[6] I urge you to choose the pursuit of holiness and purity like I have. *It is not too late.* This is the only way to live in true joy. It is the way to freedom. It is the only way to live in true happiness, and God's grace is available to help you walk out this decision.

WHY HOLINESS?

...Be holy, for I am holy (1 Peter 1:16).

God calls us to holiness because He is holy. In being holy, He has the highest, most pleasurable and exhilarating quality of life in existence. He wants to share this life with us. Therefore, He called us to enjoy the liberty of holiness. Many see holiness only as the drudgery of self-denial.[7]

But there is so much more to this. Holiness and purity are enjoyable to your heart. It is a heart that has peace and rest. Being holy is freedom, not drudgery.

GREAT GRACE

The grace of God that brings salvation has appeared... teaching us that, denying ungodliness and worldly lusts, we should live...godly in the present age... (Titus 2:11-12).

It is an impossible feat to talk about the pursuit of holiness without talking about God's grace. The love of God releases us not only from our sins, but also from the negative affects our sin has had upon our fellowship with Him. When we sincerely repent; in one sweeping act of forgiveness, He promises to not even remember what we did wrong. This is breathtaking salvation. Grace is receiving what we did not deserve: the impartation of something positive (God's power that enables us to obey Him). Grace inspires us to repent or to come into agreement (realignment) with God's heart.

But where sin increased, grace increased all the more, so that, just as sin reigned in death, so also grace might reign through righteousness to bring eternal life through Jesus Christ our Lord (Romans 5:20b-21 NIV).

The grace of God sometimes requires us to tear our hearts apart to find and search out our sin so we can be empowered (see Joel 2:12-17). The Western Church has little understanding of this. Some are confused when they say that a certain teaching "lacks grace" because it does not allow them to have confidence of God's pleasure over them until they repent.

Grace is meant to empower us to live holy lives. God's grace teaches how God intends for us to live. God's grace is given to us to do more than give us the power to live; it is also given to us to lift us *out* of sin.

One of the most misunderstood concepts in the Bible, evident in today's teaching, is that of grace. Grace has been abused and really used as an excuse to sin. Let me explain. There are three different mindsets in the Church today concerning grace:

1. Some teach a high standard of holiness yet with an impatient and intolerant God. That would define God as a "mean God."

2. Others teach low standards of holiness with a very gracious, all-accepting God. This defines God as a very "kind God."

3. The Scripture however, exhorts us to teach high standards of holiness that war against sin in our relationship with a very kind God.

God created every human being with a longing for pleasure and fascination. It is His design. Understanding this is foundational to pursuing holiness in a biblical way. The call to holiness is a call to the superior pleasures of being fascinated by the revelation of Jesus.

Holiness equips us to enjoy life together with God forever. We must not approach holiness in a negative way with gloom. We have images of strict, stubborn, joyless rules. Holiness does not keep us from pleasure, but equips us to experience it. "The power of holiness frees us from the vain imaginations of lust, pride, and bitterness."[8]

GRACE FOR REPENTANCE

Saturday mornings are set apart for family breakfasts in our home. Recently one Saturday morning, I started teaching my kids about the grace for repentance. The vital evidence of having a heart of repentance includes the fruit of repentance. The fruit of repentance has to be brought forth for repentance to be complete.

Repentance provides a doorway to reconciliation. "Each time you repent of sin, a lie that once controlled your life is broken. But if you take pleasure in wickedness, refusing God's kindness, which leads you to repentance, God eventually will give you over to the deception your rebellion has demanded."[9]

Francis Frangipane writes: "Do not despise repentance. Every season of significant spiritual growth in your walk with God will be precipitated by a time of deep repentance."[10]

True repentance is rare and leads to restored fellowship with God and others. Let me describe the process here:

1.   *Look at it* (see Ps. 51:2): Looking *straight on* at the sin committed is the first step. Human nature immediately wants to deter, hide, or "push it under the rug" as if the sin was never committed. The best way to start this process is by looking at what happened and comparing our heart, motives, and actions to the light of His Word. We can find ways to justify our actions, but if compared or measured in light of His Word, nothing is ever hidden.

2.   *Remorse* (see 2 Cor. 7:9-10): Godly remorse is the grief that comes because we know that we have lost God's approval in an area of our lives. Godly sorrow or remorse leads to repentance. Godly remorse leads to life and protection from deceiving ourselves.

3.   *Ownership* (see Gen. 3:12-13; Rom. 12:3): Jesus refuses to forgive those who ask for forgiveness, if they refuse to repent (*i.e.,* Esau, Saul, Cain). Taking

ownership of sin is one of the hardest things to do. Adam, Eve, Esau, Saul, and many others tried to pass off responsibility for their actions. This is something we must always be on guard against. We are responsible for our actions and choices in every situation.

4. *Confession* (see 1 John 1:9; Prov. 28:13): God promises mercy and purification for those who confess their sins and humble themselves before the Lord and others. You cannot fool God. He sees real brokenness and He cannot deny such a state.

5. *Quality decision* (see Ps. 4:4; Ps. 119:8): The Bible makes it clear time and again that we have free will and choice in whether we sin or not. We must make a decision, like David did, that we *will not* sin. We set our heart, mind and soul on loving God with our whole being by obeying His commandments. In the areas we have sinned we simply decide to set our hearts to "turn around" and go toward God in His ways again. Many people deceive themselves thinking that by confessing a sin they are done with it, but they are not done until they decide not to do that sin anymore. It is up to us to make a quality decision.

6. *Repent* (see Matt. 3:8): Repentance is twofold; it means to turn around and go the other direction; to change our mind. Repentance is a choice we make; we come to that choice by having godly sorrow. This sorrow leads to a change of actions that will show "fruit" in a life of true repentance.

7. *Receive His forgiveness* (see Isa. 43:23): Forgiveness is a gift that comes when we repent. We cannot earn

it; we can do nothing to get it except true repentance and humility before the Lord. He freely gives it! When Jesus shed His blood for us it was final and complete, wiping away our sin when we take hold of its benefits. (see Ps. 103). He did it for His own sake because He desired that we be with Him (see John 17:26). He wanted freedom for us; the ability for us to walk forgiven and free, to be holy and washed so we can come closer to Him.

There are some other important key steps in walking in grace for repentance. One is being quick to repent. Another is understanding that when we sincerely and wholeheartedly pursue God, sin will become less and less of an issue. The reason is our increased awareness of sin and its destructive consequences.

We can walk in full obedience to God by walking in all the light He gives us. When we fail, we simply get up again, repent, push *delete,* and return to right standing with God.

True believers do not look for excuses or scriptures to back their sin. They compare their lives to the Word and make changes out of their love for God. They know these truths: We do not need to walk in condemnation. We are encouraged to come boldly to the throne of grace and run *to* God in our weakness and sin. (See Romans 8:1; Hebrews 4:16.)

David is a great example of this. He followed the steps above with no waiting process or "purgatory." He understood that God delighted in Him, and he had confidence to come boldly before Him and not let his life be dictated by shame and condemnation.

There is a process in repentance. First, God gives us light (illumination) that convicts us of sin or draws our heart to Him (see John 6:44). Secondly, we respond by repenting or by resolving to declare war against that particular sin. Thirdly, God responds to our response by releasing more spiritual blessing in our heart (i.e. progressive victory over that particular sin). Real heart repentance always and eventually results in a progressive change in our character.

We can live lives of victory in Christ following the Lordship of Christ in every area. God is waiting for us to run to Him like the father of the prodigal son waited for his son (see Luke 15). The father saw him a long way off and ran to him. He was waiting for his son!

God does the same with us. We can have that same assurance that He enjoys us, even in our weakness, after we sincerely repent. Our repentance, obedience, and love for God can be sincere while we are still weak and fragile. Grace gives us confidence that we can have a new beginning with God after we repent. Know that God disciplines His immature children whom He enjoys (see Heb. 12:5-11).

BATTLE AT THE GATES

...And for strength to those who turn back the battle at the gate (Isaiah 28:6).

As believers we are promised strength for turning back the battle at the gates. We have three main gates that we must be vigilant to guard in order to have victory over sin in our lives. These three gateways feed our appetites of desire. They are our ears, our speech, and our eyes. Let's break down each of them. We will begin with speech and the power of words.

POWER OF WORDS

For we all stumble in many things. If anyone does not stumble in word, he is a perfect man, able also to bridle the whole body (James 3:2).

James teaches a strong concept: if we focus on our speech we can control all of our physical appetites. He gives us some helpful insights into overcoming addictions by indicating that we can bridle our whole body.

Many of us do not focus enough on the power of our words. We release life and death with each word we speak. We can unleash the very flames of hell itself (see James 3:6). When we speak words that are not in agreement with the heart of God over a situation, an individual, or a circumstance, we are releasing death. There is no in-between. Words have great power. Many of our problems would be solved if we would tame our tongues and start being more sensitive to the Holy Spirit. There are real answers to dullness in our spiritual life. One of the main answers is related to our speech.

GUARDING OUR EARS

Do not be deceived, God is not mocked; for whatever a man sows, that he will also reap. For he who sows to his flesh will of the flesh reap corruption, but he who sows to the Spirit will of the Spirit reap everlasting life (Galatians 6:7-8).

The principle of sowing and reaping is a basic and foundational law of life. The bottom line is this: it's the little things that we give ourselves over to that eventually take root and become reality in our lives, whether good or bad. We may think it's not that important and we surely don't think that the small things will have a significant effect, but the Bible says that we will reap what we sow!

One thing we often carelessly let into our ears is *music*. Is music designed solely for worship, or did God also intend music to be soothing or entertaining? The most famous musician in the Bible, King David, primarily used music for the purpose of worshiping God. (See the musical instructions recorded in the openings of Psalms 4, 6, and

55, for example.) However, when evil spirits tormented King Saul, he would call on David to play the harp in order to soothe him (see 1 Sam. 16:14-23). The Israelites also used musical instruments to warn of danger (see Neh. 4:20) and to surprise and defeat their enemies (see Judges 7:16-22).

In the New Testament, the apostle Paul instructs Christians to encourage one another with music: *"speaking to one another in psalms and hymns and spiritual songs, singing and making melody in your heart to the Lord."* (Eph. 5:19). One of the greatest tools God has given us is singing to one another and to Him and singing the Word of God. As we do that, He promises to fill us with the Holy Spirit. We want to be filled with His Spirit and not the spirit of this age.

The lifestyle that secular music artists live and promote is full of sexual immorality. This same well inspires much of their music. Often, they make their music while under the influence of demonic episodes. Then people sing the words in their songs and record companies pay them a lot of money.

People have said to me, "I can handle it. I am strong or stronger than most." The truth is that they may just have given themselves over so much to secular media that they are numb and don't feel the effects anymore. However, the consequence for a dull spirit is still there, whether they realize it or not.

I have heard the argument that there are Christian artists who are not living according to biblical standards. I am not disputing that, but the main questions should be: how does this music move me? Does it take me toward God? Does it exalt Him? Are we worshiping Him? Does it offend the Holy Spirit within me? Even if there is music that is permissible, is it beneficial? And, what do I want; what am I aiming for?

I have seen people moved with great emotion in concerts and other events, where it is evident that the Holy Spirit is not present.

This begs the question: what spirit is moving them? What is moving their hearts if it is not God?

I want to be moved by God's Spirit, only His Spirit, and not any other spirit. I want to worship God with all of my being: body, soul, and spirit. I do not want to be dulled or discipled by the spirit of this age. I want to live much higher.

One of my life visions is to be an extravagant lover of God. I will remove anything that hinders my love for Him or how I am able to receive from Him. I was created to worship Him and only Him. My emotions were made to be moved by His Spirit.

I charge you to ask the Holy Spirit about what you allow in your ears. Does it quench Him or propel Him to move in your life? Let's not live by what are considered to be acceptable standards in our society or culture, but with what will catapult us into the depths of knowing God.

FIGHT FOR THE EYES

The lamp of the body is the eye. Therefore, when your eye is good, your whole body also is full of light. But when your eye is bad, your body also is full of darkness (Luke 11:34).

The last gate is our eye. At the end of this chapter, I will invite you to make a Purity Covenant with me. This will include our speech, ears, and eyes. I believe this decision made unto God, with the power of His grace, will be life-changing. But first, let's deal with the eye gate.

Where your eyes go, your body goes; therefore your life goes the same way. What do you spend your time looking at? What do you spend your time worshiping—the Creator God or creation? What we look at with our eyes becomes the meditation of our thoughts and heart (fascination).

...Whoever looks at a woman [or man] *to lust for her* [him] *has already committed adultery with her* [him] *in his heart. If your right eye causes you to sin, pluck it out...for it is more profitable for you that one of your members perish, than for your whole body to be cast into hell* (Matthew 5:28-29).

When men and women gaze with lust, they are committing adultery in their hearts. We are supposed to be radical, so if your eye causes you to sin, pluck it out. Now, to clarify, the verse does not mean you should literally pluck out your eye. The verse is saying: "go to extreme measures to change the situation that is inflaming your heart in lust and sexual immorality."

The progression of adultery goes like this: Eye adultery is where it begins. Then it grows into heart adultery, and then physical adultery. We look, we see, and we stare. That is how the human heart works. Eye adultery grows into heart adultery by entertaining thoughts, fantasies, or imaginations.

Heart adultery can lead to physical adultery. People do not commit physical adultery by accident. They commit it as the end result of giving themselves over to more subtle secret thoughts of sexual involvement. James clearly defines the process for us:

But each one is tempted when he is drawn away by his own desires and enticed. Then, when desire has conceived, it gives birth to sin; and sin, when it is full-grown, brings forth death (James 1:14-15).

COVENANT WITH OUR EYES

We can refuse to defile the eye gate, as Job did:

I have made a covenant with my eyes; why then should I look upon a young woman?...If my heart has been enticed

by a woman, or if I have lurked at my neighbor's door...
(Job 31:1,9).

Job made a covenant with his eyes, saying, in essence, "Why should I look at a young woman with lust in my heart?" When he talked about being secretly enticed or lurking at the neighbor's door, he meant staying around with the intention to stare lustfully.

It is much easier to shut the eye gate to the realm of immorality than to put out the raging fire of immoral desires once they are burning in our lives. We have to shut the door at the entry point—the eye gate. We must turn our eyes away. If we do not diligently guard our eyes from the images seen daily on the Internet or television, then the eye gate is open to sin and we are in danger. It is not OK. It is dangerous in a very, very serious way because, if we do not make a covenant with our eyes, our imagination will be defiled and eventually destroyed.

I have also made a covenant based on Job 31:1. I have added a sevenfold commitment that I invite you to make with me and countless others before the Lord.

The first four commitments are related to confessions of sin. Commitments five, six, and seven are the follow-through actions related to those confessions. I encourage you to get around a community of friends and family to help you with this decision. There is great freedom when groups of people support each other in commitments like this. I have seen whole churches get involved. It can become a very powerful aid in keeping a purity covenant before the Lord.

I believe this is one of the best ways we can remove hindrances to our love and fellowship with the Lord.

PURITY COVENANT

Here are the seven commitments. All but the second one are from Mike Bickle's list in "Purity Covenant: 7 Practical Commitments".[11]

- *Commitment #1:* I commit to refuse to participate in *conversations* that promote immorality or make light of it. If I do engage in such conversation, I will confess my sin to those with whom I was conversing.

- *Commitment #2:* For men and women: I commit to wear modest clothing that in no way promotes sensuality. I will "occasionally" ask a godly believer who does not dress the same way I do, whether my clothing is too revealing (too tight, too short, etc.).

- *Commitment #3:* I commit to using technology (software) that promotes wisdom and safety via accountability while using my computer or electronic device. I will use this technology whether or not pornography is an area of struggle in my life.

- *Commitment #4:* I commit to choose a friend to whom I will be accountable. I commit to hold my friend's failures in *strict confidentiality.* If I break confidence, I commit to confess my indiscretion to the person whose privacy I violated. I will also repent to anyone with whom I shared the information.

- *Commitment #5:* If I "repeatedly" commit immorality, I will demonstrate true repentance by going with my friend to *confess my sin to my leadership.* I will then accept and implement the boundaries they prescribe.

- *Commitment #6:* I commit to *share with the leadership* if my friend "repeatedly" stumbles in immorality. Before doing so, I will tell my friend what I plan to do and attempt to convince my friend to accompany me.

- *Commitment #7:* For leaders: I commit to bringing those who continue in immorality to appropriate levels of discipline. I commit to *not* offering them "unsanctified mercy" instead.

I encourage you to make these commitments to the Lord, and to involve others whom you trust to help and support you.

It is my desire to provide as complete an overview in the life of holiness as possible. In closing this section, allow me to share two important truths to strengthen your pursuit of holiness. More than anything, holiness requires a posture of humility and walking in the full extent of God's grace. Let me show you the two pillars that will catapult you and strengthen you: they are the "but rather" principle and walking in the Spirit.

"BUT RATHER" PRINCIPLE

It is not only important to remove things and to make quality decisions to fight against sin, but it is also important to live in the *but rather* principle.

Although I am unmovable in my stance on the grave need to recognize, remove, and resist sin with everything in us, I also want to show the powerful *but rather* truth found throughout the New Testament. Some resist sin, but fail to live *unto* God. *Removing* and *resisting* sin go hand in hand with the *but rather* principle. Jonathan Welton illustrates this truth in his book, *Eyes of Honor.*[12]

Notice how the *but rather* principle is exemplified in Scripture:

> *Nor should there be obscenity, foolish talk or coarse joking, which are out of place, **but rather** thanksgiving* (Ephesians 5:4 NIV).

*Have nothing to do with the fruitless deeds of darkness, **but rather** expose them* (Ephesians 5:11 NIV).

*Have nothing to do with godless myths and old wives' tales; **rather**, train yourself to be godly* (1 Timothy 4:7 NIV).

…Do not live the rest of [your] *earthly lives for evil human desires, **but rather** for the will of God* (1 Peter 4:2 NIV).

***Rather**, clothe yourselves with the Lord Jesus Christ, and do not think about how to gratify the desires of the flesh* (Romans 13:14 NIV).

These verses have illustrated for us the *but rather* principle. Its focus is that we not only wage war against sin and remove the options but we also consider whom and what we should be focusing on. Our focus should look forward, toward God Himself, knowing we are empowered by the supernatural power of His grace.

WALKING IN THE SPIRIT

I say then: Walk in the Spirit, and you shall not fulfill the lust of the flesh. For the flesh lusts [wars] *against the Spirit, and the Spirit against the flesh…* (Galatians 5:16-17).

In Galatians 5:17, Paul described the violent war that is inside every believer. The flesh wars against the Spirit and the Spirit wars against the flesh.[13]

In Galatians 5:16, Paul exhorts us to "walk in the Spirit," and then gives us one of the great promises in Scripture: "You shall not fulfill the lust of the flesh." Paul did not promise us that all fleshly desire would be gone, but that we would have power to not fulfill [sinful desires]….[14]

Walking in the Spirit is within the reach of every believer. "We walk in the Spirit to the degree that we 'fellowship with Him.'"[15] One of the great benefits of the New Covenant is that at our new birth, the Holy Spirit begins to live inside us to empower us (see John 3:3-5). We experience His power most in our heart as we fellowship with Him.

> We walk in the Spirit by talking with the Spirit. The fundamental way to walk in the Spirit is by maintaining an active dialogue with the indwelling Spirit. This is key to our renewal and transformation....
>
> We will not walk in the Spirit more than we talk to the Spirit.[16]

He will help us to the degree that we talk to Him. We will obey Him more as we talk to Him. The moments that we dialogue with Him are the moments in which we are most aware of His power in our inner man.[17] We need to focus on the presence of the indwelling Holy Spirit in our war against sin. Many put their primary focus on the necessity of denying sinful desires. We walk in the Spirit or walk in the light as the condition for overcoming lust. We remove darkness by turning on the light....Light shines in the darkness, and the darkness did not comprehend (overpower) it (John 1:5).[18]

I pray that as you have read this chapter you will have been inspired to go deeper in God. The pursuit of holiness is the pursuit of God Himself. I pray that great grace abounds in your life of consecration unto the Lord.

Chapter 9

POWER BEHIND THE GREATS

*Every great movement of God can be
traced to a kneeling figure.*
—D.L. MOODY

ON JULY 7, 2006, I flew to Baltimore and went to Oriole Park at Camden Yards where the Maryland Metro Festival was being held. Franklin and Billy Graham were speaking at a three-day outreach. The excitement in the facility was electric. This was a historic weekend as Billy Graham was getting older and limiting his speaking engagements.

It had taken months of preparation for my brother Carlos who was one of the main facilitators of the Festival. Carlos had reserved upper-deck box seats in the stadium for his family. We had a great view of the entire crowd and stage.

The night was starting; there was anticipation in the air; the music began with all of its grandeur; but all of a sudden my heart leapt as my attention was taken from the stage. Suddenly, I seemed oblivious to the thousands of people around me or the excitement of the evening. I no longer cared about where everyone's attention was. I noticed that to my left next to our box seats, was Billy Graham himself. After speaking the previous night, he was sitting, enjoying the rest of the event. I was captivated. I don't think I took my eyes off him all night.

One of my heroes of faith was sitting right next to us. Even though I had briefly met him twice before, I began to think of all the questions I would like to ask him.

In this chapter we will go through the halls of history and unveil the lives of prayer and intimacy with God that some great men and women cultivated. I believe as you read these accounts (some from their very own diaries), we will glean a wealth of wisdom and be fueled into lives of prayer and the Word.

I know what these accounts did in my life, and I pray God increases His fire on yours. We will begin by looking at the life of Billy Graham.

BILLY GRAHAM

Billy Graham stands tall among the greats in the halls of history. His influence with presidents, prime ministers, kings, and queens extends beyond borders and throughout generations. The humility that he showed, while being a person of such high profile, is one of his most talked about attributes. His leadership before people and under God is truly a sign of God's favor. Billy Graham has delivered the gospel message to more people face to face than anyone in history, and has ministered on every continent of the world.

Let's look at the advice Billy Graham gives about spending time with God.

What Are the Keys to Spending Time with God?

The key is to spend time with Him. If I could give one piece of advice to a new Christian, it would be this: Develop the discipline of spending time alone with God every day. Whether you call it your quiet time or your daily devotions or some other term, there is no substitute for a daily time alone with God.

How can you develop this practice? *First, set aside a time.* Yes, it may seem impossible to find even ten extra minutes in your busy day but the real question is this: *how important is your relationship with God?* You find time for your meals and other things you think are important. Every day has exactly 1,440 minutes; can't you find even ten of them to be with your heavenly Father?

Don't wait until you have spare time; you'll probably never have any! Instead, set aside a regular time each day, a time when you are fresh and won't be interrupted (even it's only a few minutes at first). Don't wait until you're too sleepy or too preoccupied. God deserves the best minutes of our day.

Second, have a pattern. My daily quiet time always includes at least three things: *Bible reading, prayer and reflection (or meditation).* From time to time I may vary the order or spend more time on one than another, but all three are important to me. When we read the Bible, God speaks to us and we need to hear His voice. One morning I was visiting a conference center near our home and saw an old preacher reading his Bible. I spoke to him, but he didn't reply. Later, I asked if I had offended him somehow, and he said, "If I had been in prayer, talking to God, I would have spoken to you. But when I'm reading the Bible, He is speaking to me." He had a good point: When God speaks to us; He should have our full attention.

Prayer and reflection are likewise important. When we pray, we speak to God and we need to share our deepest joys and burdens with Him. When we reflect, we meditate on God's Word, and we ask God to help us apply it to our lives. Some people keep a journal to record what God is teaching them. Many also keep a prayer list, so they remember who needs their prayers (and also to record God's answers).

Finally, practice God's presence all day long. The psalmist said, "Oh, how I love Your law! I meditate on it all day long" (Psalm 119:97). The Bible tells us to "pray continually" (1 Thessalonians 5:17). When I talk with someone, I often find myself praying for them. Frequently during the day a Bible verse I read that morning will come to mind. If something unexpected comes up, I can commit it immediately to God and seek His wisdom. The Bible says, *"The Lord is near* to all who call on Him" (Psalm 145:18). Learn to practice God's presence every waking hour.[1]

EVAN ROBERTS

Many have written about Evan Roberts, including Roberts Liardon, whose book, *God's Generals*, unveiled an historical figure who was bent on giving himself to the purposes of God.

The following quote (from another source) concurs:

More than anything else, Evan Roberts was a man of prayer. Yes, the whole world felt the impact of revival that

swept Wales from November 1904 through 1905, but
certainly the extent of his public influence was a direct
result of his personal commitment to prayer. More than
100,000 Welsh people came to Christ during an unprec-
edented nine months of intense revival that closed bars
and cancelled sporting events. It triggered revival around
the world, including the famous Azusa Street revival of
1906 in Los Angeles, California, which forever changed
the landscape of Twentieth Century Christianity.

Of his early years, Evan Roberts later wrote, "I said to
myself: I will have the Spirit ... for ten or eleven years
I have prayed for revival. I could sit up all night to read
or talk about revivals. It was the Spirit who moved me
to think about revival."... It was during this period that
Evan would get so caught up in the Lord that he reported
his bed shaking. He would awaken every night at 1:00
a.m. to be "taken up into divine fellowship" and would
proceed to pray until 5:00 a.m. when he would fall back
to sleep for four hours before waking again at 9:00 a.m.
continuing in prayer until noon.

The Dawn of Revival

...In September of 1904, Roberts discovered a breakthrough as he sat listening to the evangelist Seth Joshua
plead with the Spirit to "Bend us! Bend us!" Later that
night, Roberts cried out to the Lord, "Bend me! Bend
me!" and fully surrendered to the will of God, allowing
His compassion to fill him....

He obtained approval to begin a small series of meetings that began on October 31st at a small church. This
quickly grew into a major revival that lasted two weeks.

Soon, entire communities were transformed as the meetings increased in fervor, strong moves of intercession flooding the services, often lasting well into the night.... Nine months later, Wales was in the midst of a sweeping revival that ushered in a worldwide hunger for God that would change the course of modern Christianity.

The Effect of Revival on a Nation

One eyewitness of the revival said that what drew people to Evan "perhaps more than any other thing, was the unfeigned humility in all his actions."...The newspapers began covering [his services], and the revival became a national story. Political meetings were cancelled, theaters were closed down, and bars and casinos lost their customers. Most wonderfully, Christians from all denominations worshiped together as doctrinal differences fell by the wayside. Some of the reporters themselves were converted at the meetings.[2]

SUSANNA WESLEY

Susanna Wesley is quoted as saying, *"I am content to fill a little space if God be glorified."* She was a profound figure in history, from whose life we have so much to glean. She is known as the mother of the Methodist Movement and lived from 1669-1742. During her life, Susanna Wesley faced many problems: she lost her home twice to a fire, was often left alone by her husband Samuel, and lost nine children to death, just to name a few. She remained a woman of great faith and inspiration in spite of it all.

Susanna and Samuel had nineteen children (nine of whom died in infancy). The salvation of her remaining ten children was important to her. She educated them not only in academics but also about

God. She spent time with them talking about their spiritual life on a regular basis. To her absent husband, Susanna Wesley wrote:

> I am a woman, but I am also the mistress of a large family. And though the superior charge of the souls contained in it lies upon you, yet in your long absence I cannot but look upon every soul you leave under my charge as a talent committed to me under a trust. I am not a man, nor a minister, yet as a mother and a mistress I felt I ought to do more than I had yet done. I resolved to begin with my own children; in which I observe, the following method: I take such a proportion of time as I can spare every night to discourse with each child apart. On Monday I talk with Molly, on Tuesday with Hetty, Wednesday with Nancy, Thursday with Jacky, Friday with Patty, Saturday with Charles.[3]

Though Susanna and Samuel had many marital difficulties, she never spoke ill of her husband and the fruit of their eventual reconciliation over a minor dispute that caused him to leave for nearly a year, changed history.

> The following June, I gave birth to John Benjamin Wesley, the fruit of our renewed union. We nicknamed him Jackie. He was our fifteenth child.

Though things were rough, she clung to her relationship with God. She once said:

> I will tell you what rule I observed when I was young, and too much addicted to childish diversions…never to spend more time in mere recreation in one day than I spent in private religious devotions.[4]

She reached out to those around her as well. When her husband was away she began having "church" for her children. The word spread and she began to teach over two hundred in the community, of which her husband did not approve.

Though she was fully devoted to God, she did admit that for many years she struggled with doubt and confusion about her salvation:

> ...when I had forgotten God, yet I then found He had not forgotten me. Even then He did by His Spirit apply the merits of the great Atonement to my soul, by telling me that Christ died for me.[5]

Her children record her as organizing her day amidst the busyness and home-schooling to pray two hours each day. If she could not find a space to get away alone she would throw her apron over her head for two hours and the children knew not to bother her.

Perhaps Susanna is best known *as the mother of Methodism* not just because of being the mother of John and Charles Wesley, but because of her values in knowing God. She devoted her life, in spite of her very difficult circumstances, to the cultivating of her own intimacy with the Lord and the disciplining of her children, which she often did alone. Concerning raising up children in the ways of God, she wrote:

> As soon as a child could he was taught to recite the Lord's prayer every morning and night...eventually adding the memorization of a portion of Scripture as well as other prayers.

Intimacy with the Lord was cornerstone to her life. She declared: "We must know God experientially for unless the heart perceive and know Him to be to be the supreme good, her only happiness, unless the soul feel and acknowledge that she can have no repose, no peace, no joy, but in loving and being loved by Him."[6] She was a woman with strength of character, humility, and a great example to the women and mothers of today. She was known as a woman who "underwent and overcame." Regardless of gender or position, her life provokes me. I hope that her devotion to the Lord, her tenacity to go after God under all circumstances, and her determination to teach her children to do the same, provokes you as well.

JOHN G. LAKE

No words of mine can convey to another soul the cry that was in my heart and the flame of hatred for death and sickness that the Spirit of God had stirred within me. The very wrath of God seemed to possess my soul!

These words summarized the passion that propelled the life-long ministry of John G. Lake....

By 1924, Lake was known throughout America as a leading healing evangelist.[7]

John G. Lake was known as God's "Apostle to Africa." Born in Canada in 1870, his family soon relocated to the United States, where he grew up. His healing and preaching ministry spanned the years 1898...until his death in 1935. In 1908, God sent him to Africa, where his anointed miracle ministry resulted in what has been described as "the most extensive and powerful missionary movement in all Africa."...Upon his return to America, Lake established a ministry in Spokane, Washington which resulted in no less than 100,000 astounding miracles of healing within the space of five or six years. He then established a similar work in Portland, Oregon, which also attracted widespread attention....

John G. Lake had already experienced mighty breakthroughs, powerful anointing and a real calling from God for many years before Azusa Street...and the Pentecostal

Revival.... The following is a condensed account of the spiritual hunger and preparation that Lake was taken through by God, near the beginning of the most anointed period of his ministry.[8]

John G. Lake had an amazing encounter of baptism of the Holy Spirit:

> I prayed for the Baptism of the Holy Spirit for nine months, and if a man ever prayed honestly, and sincerely in the faith, I did....I was so hungry to pray, so I went with all intentions of praying for the rest, but I had not been praying five minutes until the light of God began to shine around me, I found myself in a center of an arc of light ten feet in diameter, the whitest light in all the universe. So white! Oh how it spoke of purity. The remembrance of that whiteness, that wonderful white-ness, has been the ideal that has stood before my soul, of the purity of the nature of God ever since.

> Then a Voice began to talk to me out of that light. There was no form. And the Voice began to remind me of this incident, and that incident of disobedience to my parents, from a child; of my obstinacy, and dozens of instances when God brought me up to the line of abso-lutely putting my body, soul, and spirit upon the altar forever. I had my body upon the altar for ten years, and I had been a minister of the Gospel. But when the Lord comes, He opens to the soul the depths that have never been touched in your life....

> My soul was crying out to God in a yearning too deep for words, when suddenly it seemed to me, that I had passed under a shower of warm tropical rain, which was

not falling upon me, but through me. My spirit, and soul and body under this influence soothed into such a deep still calm, as I had never known. My brain, which had always been so active, became perfectly still. An awe of the presence of God settled over me. I knew it was God.

Some moments passed; I do not know how many. The Spirit said, "I have heard your prayers, I have seen your tears. You are now Baptized in the Holy Spirit." Then currents of power began to rush through my being from the crown of my head to the soles of my feet. The shocks of power increased in rapidity, and voltage. As these currents of power would pass through me, they seemed to come upon my head, rush through my body, and through my feet into the floor...Even at this late date, the awe of that hour rests upon my soul. My experience has truly been as Jesus said that He shall be within you "a well of water, springing up into everlasting life." That never-ceasing fountain has flowed through my spirit, soul, and body day, and night, bringing salvation, and healing, and the Baptism of the Spirit in the power of God to multitudes.[9]

Robert Liardon cites that John "was responsible for raising over 1,000,000 converts, 625 churches and 1,250 preachers in five years of ministry."[10] In his book *God's Generals*, Roberts Liardon cites that "according to government statistics, between the years of 1915-1920, Spokane, Washington, was the 'healthiest city in the world,' because of the ministry of John G. Lake. The mayor of Spokane held a public commemoration to honor his efforts."[11] Lake continued his ministry in North America until his death in 1935. He fought an outstanding fight and ran a great race, right to the very end.

JONATHAN EDWARDS

Jonathan Edwards' own words reveal much about his relationship with God:

> The true spirit of prayer is no other than God's own Spirit dwelling in the hearts of the saints. And as this spirit comes from God, so doth it naturally tend to God in holy breathings and pantings. It naturally leads to God, to converse with him by prayer.[12]

Edwards' passion for God began in his childhood:

> Edwards sensed God's calling on his life rather early. He recorded in his journals that he spoke often about God to the other boys his age, and together they built a place to pray in the woods. He wrote that for a period of months, he and the other boys would go there as often as five times a day to seek God.[13]

Edwards was an eighteenth-century preacher "widely acknowledged to be America's most important and original philosophical theologian" and a great intellect. Edwards played a critical role in shaping the First Great Awakening, and oversaw some of the first revivals in 1733-35 at his church in Northampton, Massachusetts.[14]

> The First Awakening (or The Great Awakening) was a Christian revitalization movement that swept Protestant Europe and British America, and especially the American colonies in the 1730s and 1740s, leaving a permanent impact on American religion. It resulted from powerful preaching that gave listeners a sense of deep personal revelation of their need of salvation by Jesus Christ. Pulling away from ritual and ceremony, the Great Awakening made Christianity intensely personal to the average

person by fostering a deep sense of spiritual conviction and redemption, and by encouraging introspection and a commitment to a new standard of personal morality.[15]

THE LEGACY OF DAVID BRAINERD

One of the most profound heroes of faith was David Brainerd. His life was a legacy that not only inspired but his life also left a benchmark for us to attain. David Brainerd was a missionary during the 1700s. He lived an obscure life in the forests of northeast America. He was a man that opened up heaven when he prayed. He didn't gain multitudes of conversions, but the conversions he did see were of such a deep working that all of the new believers did not backslide. His gravestone reads: "Sacred to the memory of David Brainerd, the faithful and devoted missionary to the Susquehanna, Delaware and Stockbridge Indians of America, who died in this town, October 8, 1717."[16]

"He gave his life for Native Americans, spending hours in prayer for them for very little in return."[17] Brainerd's life of prayer has done much to influence modern missions.

Many great Church leaders in history have read his diary. When William Carey read it, he was set on fire for God and immediately headed off to do missions in India....

Jonathan Edwards, who hosted Brainerd in his house during Brainerd's final days (his daughter and Brainerd were to be married), said, "I praise God that it was in His providence that he should die in my house, that I might hear his prayers (for the conversion of the world), and that I might witness his consecration and that I might be inspired by his example."[18]

John Wesley wrote, "Find preachers of David Brainerd's spirit and nothing can stand before them. But without this, what will gold or silver do? No more than lead or iron." "What can be done to revive this nation? Let every man carefully read the life of David Brainerd."[19] Reading about what others said about David Brainerd is powerful, but until you hear and look at his personal diary, you will not be pierced by the reality of this man's extraordinary heart of humility and power. His diary entries include the following:

> O my blessed God! Let me climb up near to Him, and love, and long, and plead, and wrestle, and stretch after Him, and for deliverance from the body of sin and death. Alas! My soul mourned to think I should ever lose sight of its Beloved again. O come, Lord Jesus, amen.[20]

> My soul longed for communion with Christ and for the mortification of indwelling corruption, especially spiritual pride.[21]

> [I] was enabled to plead with fervency for the advancement of Christ's kingdom in the world and to intercede for dear absent friends. At noon, Christ enabled me to wrestle with Him and to feel, as I trust, the power of divine love in prayer.... to prepare me for the work of the ministry, to give me divine aid and direction in my preparations for that great work, and in His own time to send me into His harvest. I endeavored to plead for the divine presence for the day, and not without some life. In the forenoon, I felt the power of intercession for immortal souls; for the advancement of the kingdom of my dear Lord....[22]

> My very soul pants for the complete restoration of the blessed image of my Saviour, that I may be fit for the blessed enjoyments and employments of the heavenly world.[23]

God was pleased to pour such ineffable comforts into my soul that I could do nothing for some time but say over and over, "O my sweet Saviour! O my sweet Savior! Whom have I in heaven but Thee? And there is none upon earth, that I desire beside Thee."...Oh, that my soul might never offer any dead, cold, services to my God![24]

I scarce ever launched so far into the eternal world, as then. I got so far out on the broad ocean that my soul with joy triumphed over all the evils on the shores of mortality.[25]

The Impact of Brainerd's Preaching

Here are some comments on the impact of David Brainerd's preaching:

The divine truths were attended with a surprising influence, and produced a great concern among them. There were scarce three in forty that could refrain from tears and bitter cries. They all at once, seemed in agony of soul to obtain an interest in Christ; and the more I discoursed of the love and compassion of God in sending His Son to suffer for the sins of men; and the more I invited them to come and partake of His love, the more their distress was aggravated, because they felt themselves unable to come. It was surprising to see how their hearts seemed to be pierced with the tender and melting invitations of the gospel, when there was not a word of terror spoken to them.[26]

I stood amazed at the influence that seized the audience almost universally, and could compare it to nothing more aptly than the irresistible force of a mighty torrent, or swelling deluge, that with it insupportable weight and pressure bears down and sweeps before it whatever is in its way. Almost all persons of all ages were bowed down with concern together, and scarce one was able to withstand the shock of this surprising operation. Old men and women, who had been drunken wretches for many years, and some little children, not more than six or seven years of age, appeared in distress for their souls.... And it was apparent these children were not merely frightened with seeing the general concern; but were made sensible of their danger, the badness of their hearts, and their misery without Christ....

The most stubborn hearts were now obliged to bow.... They were almost universally praying and crying for mercy, in every part of the house, and many out of doors, and numbers could neither go nor stand.[27]

I had not discoursed long before their concern rose to a great degree, and the house was filled with cries and groans. And when I insisted on the compassion and care of the Lord Jesus for those that were lost, who thought themselves undone, and could find no way of escape, this melted them down the more and aggravated their distress that they could not find and come to so kind a Saviour.[28]

The spirit of intercession and passion for souls that David Brainard had is perhaps unparalleled in all of history. I hope as you read these accounts that your heart was awakened to what could be, and inflamed with a passion like that of this man.

CLOSING

Oh, to have the opportunity to walk through the halls of history and to spend an hour with these extraordinary people. I trust that the time we've spent with these great heroes of faith has inspired you to pursue the higher call of God on your life and to walk in the power they walked in.

Chapter 10

FOLLOWING OUR FATHERS

*...The people who know their God shall be
strong, and carry out great exploits.*
—DANIEL 11:32

SUCCESS IS OFTEN viewed as a set of accomplishments or titles. Even though this has been society's measurement for success, it is incomplete. *True success is to know and love God and to be known and loved by Him.* Athletes and musicians who have garnered trophies and achievements, often feel emptiness that no award or hall of fame can satisfy. After fame and fortune and being known by so many, the loneliness remains.

In the same way, after all our accomplishments and good things we do and even the failures we make; true success is measured in knowing why we were created, to know our Creator and to love Him completely.

Success and favor really only come from knowing God. In all that we do, if our identity is firmly established in knowing God, it really doesn't matter how big the crowds get or how small they are. It really doesn't matter how big our businesses become or how small they stay. It does not matter who knows us and who we know. When we are firmly established in knowing the Creator of the universe, and have the assurance that He knows us, we already have achieved real success.

Having said all of this, God still has a plan, a destiny and assignment for us to accomplish. He has given each of us gifts for us to act upon to the best of our ability, and to make a great impact with His favor and success.

Let's look at a few examples on how to attain and maintain great success. Acts 2:42 describes how the believers walked: *"They devoted themselves to the apostles' teaching and to fellowship, to the breaking of bread and to prayer"* (NIV).

Then Acts 3:1 says: *"One day Peter and John were going up to the temple at the time of prayer—at three in the afternoon"* (NIV). Here we see a glimpse into the lifestyle of prayer that the apostles walked in. In the midst of starting the Church, they gave themselves to prayer and the Word. They walked in great power and authority; such power the world has never seen. Everywhere they went, miraculous things happened. This was a common thing for them and this can be common still. This is what I call *normal* Christianity. No matter what vocation of life you're in, whether you're in the marketplace, the ministry, school, or stay-at-home parenting, full power is available to you. Great success can be yours.

DANIEL

Then I set my face toward the Lord God to make request by prayer and supplications, with fasting, sackcloth, and ashes (Daniel 9:3).

Young Daniel was carried off to Babylon where he became famous for interpreting dreams, and rose to become one of the most important figures of his time. Daniel, the Hebrew prophet in exile, gives us a portrait of a real, weak human being who, when confronted with the difficult options, time and time again purposed in his heart to give himself to the Lord in secret.

Daniel is not meant to be viewed merely as a historical rarity; rather, he is a prototype of how God is calling us to live. The life of faithfulness that Daniel lived should be viewed as an invitation to anyone and everyone who will heed its call.

The content of the Book of Daniel, including the visions and dreams, along with the lifestyle portrayed by Daniel himself, is actually more relevant to this generation than it was even to Daniel in his day and the generations that followed him soon thereafter.

It is clear that even before he was taken captive to Babylon that Daniel was raised in a godly environment of prayer and fasting that became the groundwork for his resisting the spirit of Babylon. This type of upbringing put steel in his spirit to refuse the seductions of the world. We must ask the obvious question that is often neglected: *Who were Daniel's father and mother?* or *What was the environment in which he was raised?* It is very clear that Daniel was prepared beforehand for the hour of trouble.

Daniel 1:8 tells us that Daniel *"purposed in his heart that he would not defile himself...."* Clearly, Daniel settled the issue once and for all of whether or not he would betray God. This does not mean that Daniel did not face temptations or struggle through his decisions, but it shows us the power and strength of a purposed heart to refuse compromise in worldliness and to live holy. Many of us are left to our own devices to resist sin because we do not submit to the grace of God in operation through the Holy Spirit to actually purpose in our hearts, as Daniel did, to *not* defile ourselves.

From his early days Daniel embraced a lifestyle of prayer (see Dan. 6:10) and fasting (see Dan. 1:8). Fasting reminds us that one's spirit, soul, and body are connected and cannot be separated.

Now when Daniel learned that the decree had been published, he went home to his upstairs room where the windows opened toward Jerusalem. Three times a day he got down on his knees and prayed, giving thanks to his God, just as he had done before (Daniel 6:10 NIV).

I love the discipline that Daniel shows us. Even facing persecution and death, he prayed on his knees three times a day. He gave thanks as a regular pattern. Daniel sustained his prayer life with passion for decades, from about age sixteen to eighty-two.

This is one of the greatest strengths of Daniel; but it can also be one of our greatest strengths. We can resolve to live a lifestyle of prayer and fasting. We can make a determined decision to love God. Our response to His love starts as a choice to have a heart of affectionate obedience. We should regularly realign our hearts, intentionally renewing our vision to make loving Him our first priority, and to go deep in God.

In our quest to go deep in God, fasting quickens our spiritual appetites, sharpens our spiritual discernment, combats our trust in our own strength, and weakens the cravings of our flesh such as nothing else does. Overeating and overindulgence cause the spirit to grow dim and dull. Spiritual sharpness is diminished, and spiritual discernment wanes. Daniel wanted his spiritual discernment to be strong as he entered his Babylonian enslavement. He needed all of his spiritual wits about him in such a culture absent of God.

Moreover, fasting is one of the divine escorts that produce in us a longing for Jesus. As John Piper puts it in his book, *Hunger for God: "The birthplace of Christian fasting is homesickness for God."*[1] In fasting, we deny ourselves the legitimate pleasures of this age for the superior pleasures of knowing and encountering God. Fasting does not "buy" us anything except to gloriously position our hearts to receive revelation and wisdom (see Matt. 6:18). Daniel and his friends bore the indignation of the fasted lifestyle because they knew something else much bigger was at stake than feasting on food: their devotion and loyalty to God.

You can start now. We must not despise the day of small beginnings (see Zech. 4:10). We value the small stirrings of God's Word and Spirit on our heart. The kingdom starts as a seed in our heart and grows slowly but surely. We cannot accurately measure it during the process.

> *The kingdom of God is as if a man should scatter seed... and should sleep by night and rise by day, and the seed should sprout and grow, he himself does not know how* (Mark 4:26-27).

DAVID—THE GREAT PSALMIST OF ISRAEL

The story of King David is one of the most encouraging stories in the Bible. He was known as the man who loved God (see 1 Sam. 13:14). He was a lonely child, from a poor family who lived in a small town. In his youth, his family and friends rejected David. He had unusual insight into how his love for God moved God's heart. This is the story of how a teenage boy who was a "nobody" in man's eyes discovered that he was a "somebody" in God's eyes.

> *The LORD has sought for Himself a man after His own heart...* (1 Samuel 13:14).

The Lord *"sought"* David, and is still seeking for this type of person.

> *The eyes of the LORD run to and fro throughout the whole earth, to show Himself strong on behalf of those whose heart is loyal to Him.* (2 Chronicles. 16:9).

The importance of David's story is that it can be our story, simply by making the choices David made in his youth and in a lifetime of setting his heart on Him. We see how in the very early days of David's life as a young shepherd boy he made it a priority to be with God. He sang songs to Him, talked to Him, and was a lover of God. It is the story of how God both enjoys and uses weak and broken people who set their hearts on Him. It is the story of how God sees our heart and how we move His heart. God doesn't just love us, He likes us.

We see David throughout the psalms praying and crying out to the Lord. His prayers are among the most heart-rending, real and raw prayers. They are prayers of a man who is talking to a real God, not throwing up words to the sky and hoping God hears. He even said in Psalm 116:2: *"Because He has inclined His ear to me...."*

We need this same revelation of God's delight in us and of His ear being inclined to us. One of the great examples of David's prayer was his prayer of repentance in Psalm 51. In this prayer we see his heart-rending grief and sorrow over his sin. We also see his heart to bridge the gap his sin had caused. The great thing about David was his passion to please God and his ability to get back up again and have confidence in God's heart for him even in his weakness. This is a great example of how to live our lives with the Lord.

David found his primary identity in his relationship with God, instead of with people. David knew his identity was not in who liked him or what he accomplished before people. In Bethlehem, even in his youth, David developed a spiritual root system of intimacy with God. David was first and foremost a worshiper who longed to know God's heart.

> *One thing I have desired...All the days of my life, to behold the beauty of the LORD...* (Psalm 27:4).

More than anything else, we can learn from looking at David's life that he resolved to know God and to know His emotions. Our

God is moved by great emotion over us. His thoughts are toward us, and if we would posture our lives in the same way, we would live daily encounters with fresh revelation of who God is.

HANNAH

I love the story of Hannah. Here we see a woman who is barren, which especially in those days was very sad and painful. Much of the value placed on a woman at that time was her ability to have children, particularly sons. The story of Hannah in First Samuel chapter 1 is one that gives us a prophetic picture of today's barren Church. In our barrenness, we cry out to the Lord and He breaks in with a prophetic Spirit in our lives and nation.

Hannah was one of two wives married to a man named Elkanah. One of the wives is termed as *"having children,"* while Hannah is termed as *"having no children."* In two places in the Bible we see that *"the Lord had closed her womb"* (1 Sam. 1:5,6) although she was loved by her husband and was given a double portion in the offering.

> *But to Hannah he would give a double portion, for he loved Hannah, although the LORD had closed her womb* (1 Samuel 1:5).

The Lord had also closed her womb while the other wife who *"had children"* taunted and provoked her. This scenario year after year drove Hannah to the point of desperation. Hannah went to the temple and wept and cried out to the Lord to give her a son.

> *And her rival also provoked her severely, to make her miserable, because the LORD had closed her womb. So it was, year by year, when she went up to the house of the LORD, that she provoked her; therefore she wept and did not eat* (1 Samuel 1:6-7).

And she was in bitterness of soul, and prayed to the LORD *and wept in anguish. Then she made a vow and said, "O* LORD *of hosts, if You will indeed look on the affliction of Your maidservant and remember me, and not forget Your maidservant, but will give Your maidservant a male child, then I will give him to the* LORD *all the days of his life, and no razor shall come upon his head"* (1 Samuel 1:10-11).

The Lord gave Hannah more than a son. In a time when no one prophesied, God gave Hannah a consecrated priest and prophet who would restore the Word of the Lord in one generation. Samuel came forth when the lamp was almost out in the temple and the Word of the Lord was rare and there was no widespread revelation in the land (see 1 Sam. 3:1).

Even the fact that the Lord had closed her womb showed that He was setting her up for something far more glorious. It was not enough for Hannah to just be loved by her husband; she wanted to have children. Hannah came to a point where she quit running from her affliction. Instead, she embraced it and cried out from her depths.

We need a desperate cry today. Are we desperate in our barrenness? Are we comfortable in the state of our lives? Have we accepted the place we are in as if it will always be? I plead with you, there's so much more. Get desperate like Hannah. Cry out to Him today. There's fruit far more glorious than you could ever imagine.

The Lord heard Hannah and answered her in a powerful way. She consecrated her son Samuel to the Lord. He became a man who had the spirit of a Nazarite resting on him. He heard from the Lord, and not one of his words fell to the ground (see 1 Sam. 3:19).

It takes the Hannahs to give birth to the Samuels! Where are the Hannahs who cry out in desperation for the prophetic voice of God to be released in the land? It takes the Hannahs who get a vision to intercede and cry out and then see God change everything in one generation. Let's sign up to be Hannahs and begin to ask the Lord for a change in the land again.

JESUS—THE GREATEST EXAMPLE OF SUCCESS

During the days of Jesus' life on earth, he offered up prayers and petitions with fervent cries and tears to the one who could save him from death, and he was heard because of his reverent submission (Hebrews 5:7 NIV).

Whether it was *"very early in the morning"* (Mark 1:35 NIV) or *"all night"* long (Luke 6:12), Jesus prayed. He is our greatest example. He went from one place of prayer to the next, and in between performed many miracles. He went from another place of prayer to the next, and in between fed five thousand people.

After seeing this pattern of how Jesus walked in such power, the disciples were awestruck. They heard all of His messages, witnessed all of His miracles, saw much deliverance, and heard many gracious words. Yet they never asked to be instructed in any of these great things. They simply asked Him to teach them how to pray. They understood the correlation between His life of power and His connection with God.

What a privilege it is to learn about prayer from the One who is the greatest teacher and He who had the greatest prayer life. The prayer that Jesus taught the disciples is commonly known as "The Lord's Prayer." Let's examine it closely.

TEACH US TO PRAY

Mike Bickle helps to give some practical ways to look at the Lord's Prayer. We will study these and Jesus' own words.

In this manner, therefore, pray: our Father in heaven, hallowed be Your name (Matthew 6:9).

This magnificent prayer model Jesus taught is "based on what God is like and on the nature of the kingdom....Jesus told us the things that we must know and keep central in our quest to grow strong in prayer."[2]

> Jesus pointed out six requests to pray regularly. The first three focus on God's glory (His name, kingdom, and will). The second three focus on man's needs (physical, relational, and spiritual).[3]

The Ten Commandments are organized in a similar way with the first tablet focused on our relationship to God and the second on our relationship to people.

Praying Focusing on God's Glory

> ...*Our Father in heaven, hallowed be Your name* (Matthew 6:9).

Praying to our Father in heaven: The Father longs for a relationship with a deep partnership with us as He tenderly trains (disciplines), provides, protects, and directs us. It is an indescribable exaltation for us to have a "family" status and be heirs with Jesus in God's kingdom. This speaks to us about our identity and position.

So when we pray "Our Father," *our* means that He is not only "my" Father but also "our" Father. We pray to our Father for our daily bread, and forgiveness of our sins, and victory over our temptations, etc. Our prayer requests are tempered with realities of who we are to God as one "family" by using the word, "our." We are to pray for the whole family and not only for ourselves.

Next, we pray to *"Our Father in heaven."* "In heaven" Jesus combined two ideas about God here in these two words; this is both powerful and relational. "In heaven" points to the father's transcendence (His magnificent existence) and sovereignty. Jesus set the context with God, with His sovereignty and majesty. He combined God's fatherly love with His heavenly power. These first words cause us to be awed by "Our Father in heaven" who longs for relationship with people like us. Jesus' point was to inspire us to awe, humility and confidence.[4]

...hallowed be Your name (Matthew 6:9).

Praying for God's name to be honored: The first petition is that God's majestic name be treated and seen rightly. God's "Name" refers to His person, character, and authority. He is transcendent or wholly "other than" so we must not take God's name in vain or lightly. His name is holy and infinitely exalted. We pray that it may be hallowed or acknowledged or treated on earth as holy.[5]

As we are praying this we are asking God to break in with power to cause more people to acknowledge the truth about Him. It's His name that causes angels to move, demons to flee, and people to bend. It's His name by which we are saved and it's His character in who He is that changes our hearts and lives.

Your kingdom come. Your will be done on earth as it is in heaven (Matthew 6:10).

Praying for the kingdom to come: The second petition asks for an increase of the kingdom. The kingdom is the place God's Word is obeyed, His will is done, and His power expressed. Some examples of the kingdom being manifested are when the sick are healed and demons are cast out (Matt. 12:28).[6]

We pray for the kingdom to increase and we should not be content to serve in it without a life of prayer. The Lord gives more if we ask for more, because it develops our relationship with Him; this is what He desires.

> *...Your will be done on earth as it is in heaven* (Matthew 6:10).

God's will being done: The third request includes our personal obedience in context to God's kingdom purposes. His will consists of His commandments and our ministry assignment. We should seek to learn all that we can about God's will by first studying the Scriptures. His Word is His will. We should also seek to know what God is doing in our generation and then throw ourselves fully into it.[7]

PRAYING FOR OUR PERSONAL NEEDS

There is a well-known saying that goes like this: *Seek His face and not His hand.* That is completely wrong and misunderstood. We should seek His face *and* His hand, but in the right order: His face first and then His hand.

Some conclude that prayer should never include selfish things so they neglect to make personal petitions. Jesus commanded us to bring our personal needs to God in prayer.[8] Three requests in the prayer are personal...

> ...for our needs—physical (daily bread), relational (forgiveness), and spiritual (deliverance from evil). These

prayers express our dependence on God in every area of life.[9]

Give us this day our daily bread. And forgive us our debts, as we forgive our debtors (Matthew 6:11-12).

Our daily bread is the fourth request: "[It] is for our *daily* provision, protection, and direction"[10] (spiritual and physical). The bread here refers to all our natural needs.

We do not pray to inform God of our needs (Matt. 6:7-8), but to enhance our relationship with Him. Asking God for our needs does not free us from the responsibility of working.[11]

For even when we were with you, we commanded you this: If anyone will not work, neither shall he eat (2 Thessalonians 3:10).

And forgive us our debts, as we forgive our debtors (Matthew 6:12).

Being forgiven and forgiving: The fifth petition concerns our relationship with God and people.[12] The proof that we have been freely forgiven is that we have the ability and willingness to gladly forgive others. The man who knows he has been forgiven is full of gratefulness and is compelled to forgive others.[13]

And lead us not into temptation, but deliver us from the evil one (Matthew 6:13 NIV; see also RSV).

Lead us, not into temptation but to the place of escape: The sixth petition has caused much discussion. Since "God never tempts anyone with evil (Jas. 1:13),"[14] why do we need to ask Him to lead us not into temptation? The reason we pray this is so that God leads us to *escape* from tempting situations. There is always a way out. He knows what it is and will show us if we ask Him.

Many agree that in this passage Jesus was using a figure of speech to "express one petition in two ways—*lead us from temptation* and *deliver us from* evil. The second half of the request defines positively what the first half expresses negatively."[15] Jesus urged the apostles to pray that they not "enter into temptation (Matt. 26:41; Luke 22:40). To enter temptation speaks of something far more intense than the general temptations we all face. It points to a specific 'storm' attacking us.[16] It is the time "when three components come together—when demonic activity…is heightened, our lusts are aroused, and circumstances are optimum for sin."[17] *"Watch and pray, lest you enter into temptation. The spirit indeed is willing, but the flesh is weak"* (Matt 26:41).

There are strategic times when demonically heightened temptations come against us all of a sudden like a great storm. Praying before "the storm" of temptation expresses our need for Him that depends on God's strength as we acknowledge our weakness. These "pre-temptation prayers" for help act as a preemptive strike countering the enemy's assault against us. We can reduce the temptation by praying.[18] I hope this gives you an understanding of the Lord's Prayer. And, as you have taken a little closer look at how some of our fathers lived their lives of intimacy with God, I hope you have been fueled to pursue your own life of intimacy with a new resolve. These are the ways of the kingdom and it is not far from the reach of any one of us.

Chapter 11

CULTIVATING A SUPERNATURAL PRAYER LIFE

I thank my God I speak with
tongues more than you all…
—THE APOSTLE PAUL, I Corinthians 14:18

POWER. REAL POWER. There is a power to which even bolts of lightning cannot be compared. There is a power available to you that will change your life forever. It's the power of the uncreated God.

If you want to live a life of victory and power, I invite you to embark on a journey with me and search out the mysteries of God. I invite you to cultivate a supernatural prayer life that is only found by praying in tongues.

In January 2010, God started challenging my prayer life. Up to this time, I had mostly prayed using the Word of God as my dialogue. I prayed biblical prayers, trying my best to be in line with

His Word. I had prayed in tongues only on rare occasions or in special meetings; my personal prayer time was rarely devoted to praying in tongues.

God began inviting me to go deeper with Him. He was calling me to expand my spirit man and my understanding of the Scriptures related to the necessity and benefits of praying in tongues.

Now I am fully aware that the Church in many ways has placed praying in tongues on the fringe for certain sects or groups, or has considered it a thing of the past. But I am more convinced, not only that this gift is available to all Christians today, but also that it is the kick-start to all spiritual gifts available to every believer.

If you really want to experience supernatural power in your prayer life, praying in tongues is a must. The best news I have for you is that this gift is available to you as a Christian today. The gift of tongues is one you already possess within you if you are a believer, because *"His divine power has given to us all things that pertain to life and godliness..."* (2 Pet. 1:3).

Even if you do not presently speak in tongues, you have access to this gift by the power of the Holy Spirit. It is like having a wealthy uncle who gave you a million-dollar check, but if you do not cash it in, you do not have it. Because the Holy Spirit lives within you, you can decide to access this incredible gift and it is yours. It's as simple as that. And even though tongues may not yet be manifested, that does mean you do not have it. Not perceiving a thing does not imply it is not there. It only means the gift is not in use because it has not yet been activated.

Praying in tongues has been the greatest empowerment and avenue to supernatural encounter for me on a daily basis. As I have increased praying in tongues, I have grown in more ways than I can comprehend. It has literally changed my life. It has expanded my ability to receive the greater depths of God in my life. Praying in tongues has changed my emotions. Praying in tongues has changed how I read the Bible. Praying in tongues has changed how I speak. By praying in tongues, I have encountered God in my spirit man more than any other single thing in my life.

BUILDING YOURSELF UP

But you, beloved, building yourselves up on your most holy faith, praying in the Holy Spirit... (Jude 20).

"Praying in the Spirit" means that our spirits are praying into the Spirit of God—the Spirit who searches the depths of God, the Spirit who knows all the things of God. As we are praying into the Spirit of God, we are, so to speak, turning on a flashlight in our souls and going on a treasure hunt with God. The thoughts of God, the mind of God, and the presence of God are at our disposal through His Spirit, and speaking in tongues turns on the light to see what is already available. When we pray in tongues we are building ourselves up.

We are so to speak, charging ourselves up, like charging a battery. We are building, fortifying, and strengthening our faith by praying in tongues—or as Jude calls it, praying in the Spirit.

THE WAYS OF GOD

Most people don't pray in tongues because it's foolishness to them. The mysteries of God do not necessarily make sense to our natural minds. Our God, who hung on the cross, a Savior who was born of a virgin, wrote a book, using forty different authors. The book was written by human hands, in two different languages which we believe is the Word of God.

As you can see, the ways of the kingdom are opposite to how the world operates and thinks. Other ways of the kingdom include: it's better to give than to receive; we are to forgive rather than keep offense; whoever wants to be the greatest must be a servant; and water baptism represents new birth (see Acts 20:35; Mark 11:25; Matt. 23:11; Mark 16:16).

I could go on and on with examples of things that are God's wisdom, but foolishness to man. These are the ways of God. We must have faith in God's Word that we are building ourselves up by speaking in tongues, trading our own might for God's might. Everything in the kingdom of God is accessed by faith. Most of the time we have to deal with unbelief in order to take a hold of the ways of the kingdom of God. Praying in tongues is accessed the same way, through faith.

TONGUES ARE FOR EVERYONE

I wish you all spoke with tongues… (1 Corinthians 14:5).

The apostle Paul wanted *everyone* to speak in tongues. Why? Because it edifies *us* when we pray in tongues. There is a personal benefit that we receive when we pray in tongues (the private form of tongues).

Later on in this chapter I will explain the different operations of tongues. All born-again believers can access the private form of tongues (tongues to God) to build their inner man. There is another form of tongues that the Holy Spirit gives, as He wills, (tongues to men that must be accompanied by interpretation).

Paul explained in First Corinthians 14:4 that all Christians, even in modern times, benefit from praying in tongues, and that's why the Bible tells us to *"pray in the Spirit on all occasions"* (Eph. 6:18 NIV).

As a believer of Jesus Christ, you have everything that you need, *"Therefore you do not lack any spiritual gift as you eagerly wait for our Lord Jesus Christ to be revealed"* (1 Cor. 1:7 NIV). There is another reason why Paul desired that everyone prayed in tongues.

PRAYING TO GOD

For he who speaks in a tongue does not speak to men but to God, for no one understands him; however, in the spirit he speaks mysteries (1 Corinthians 14:2).

When we pray in tongues, we convey the glorious acts of God. This Bible verse says everything for me. The key here is that when we pray in tongues, in our private prayer language, we are praying to God and not to men.

I believe the Word of God. If it says I speak mysteries when I pray in tongues, I am confident that I speak mysteries. When I pray in tongues, I am praying out glorious secrets and treasures that are hidden for me to discover.

When we speak in tongues, our spirit stands side by side with the Holy Spirit, laying hold of all the promises of God regarding our inheritance in Christ Jesus.

For with stammering lips and another tongue He will speak to this people, to whom He said, "This is the rest with which You may cause the weary to rest," and, "This is the refreshing"... (Isaiah 28:11-12).

Moreover, God gave the gift of tongues to all believers for spiritual rest and refreshing, and to circumvent the effects of weariness and stress. We are spiritual beings, but live in physical bodies. Our Western mindsets place a high priority on rest and relaxation, but true rest is only found in our spirit man; then our physical man will follow suit. Most of us are getting beat up because we are primarily directed by our emotions rather than by the Spirit of God. God wants us to build our most holy faith through praying in tongues.

I have experienced many times when I am either physically tired or coming against a difficult situation. Ten out of ten times, when I pray in tongues, I come out victorious. My situation may not have changed immediately and my physical body may not be rested, but regardless of all of that, my spirit becomes stronger, more focused, and aligned with Him, and I am given the right direction and path to take. I have even experienced times when discouragement or depression has tried to get a hold of my life, and as I pray in tongues, the opposite occurs. The kingdom of heaven becomes my new reality. I have joy instead of depression. I get peace instead of turmoil. I get faith instead of fear. I access the kingdom of God instead of the ways of the earthly natural realm. I get to see from God's perspective instead of my earthly perspective.

Now this excites me! I want this power in my life more than ever! I hope you do, too.

ROADBLOCKS TO PRAYING IN TONGUES

To receive this spiritual language of praying in tongues, first of all, we must understand that we cannot earn it. There is no need for striving, begging, or wondering if you can receive it, because it is already within us as born-again believers.

This is a literal gift. All we have to do is open it and access it. God wants us to have this prayer language. The power of the Holy Spirit can be accessed freely; all we have to do is receive it and take hold of it.

There has been much confusion between the gifts of the Spirit given by the Spirit for specific times *for the edification of the Church,* and the private forms of tongues which are *for living by the Spirit on a daily basis.* I will address a few confusing and misunderstood activities of the Spirit:

Prophecy

The gift of prophecy is a gift from the Holy Spirit which falls on you for the edification of the Church for a specific time and moment. People can operate in the gift of prophecy to speak edification, exhortation, and comfort to men (see 1 Cor. 14:3). This is *not* to be confused with the *prophetic spirit*, which we can walk in daily as we tap into the mind of Christ within us. We are *all* to pursue prophecy.

> *Pursue love, and desire spiritual gifts, but especially that you may prophesy* (1 Corinthians 14:1).

Healing

For those who are sick, God gives the gift of healing; and some are given a supernatural gift by the Lord for healing the sick. As with the other gifts, this gift is *not* to be confused with the power that we all carry to pray for the sick in *every circumstance* and *opportunity*. We can be vessels to release the healing that Jesus already paid for. Psalm 103:2-3 states: *"Forget not all His benefits—who forgives all your sins and heals all your diseases"* (NIV). We have already been healed by what Jesus paid for on the cross. God calls us to lay hands on the sick and they will recover (see James 5:14).

Speaking in Tongues

There is a gift of tongues that is given by the Spirit for the edification of the Church, *with* the interpretation of tongues. This should *not* be confused with our *devotional prayer language of tongues*. The first is a gift for a time and moment in the presence of, and for the benefit of other people. It is given *with* the interpretation of tongues so that those in attendance can understand what is being said. The second is for *daily life* and personal edification to be used anytime and all the time (as discussed earlier). The personal prayer language of tongues is a great way to *"pray without ceasing"* (1 Thess. 5:17).

> *Therefore let him who speaks in a tongue pray that he may interpret* (1 Corinthians 14:13).

Faith

We are all called to walk and pray in faith, using the measure of faith that the Bible tells us God has given to us (see Rom. 12:3). We can cultivate greater levels of faith by hearing and meditating on the Word of God.

"So then faith comes by hearing, and hearing by the word of God" (Rom. 10:17). The Holy Spirit gives supernatural endowment of faith for "walking on water" moments. I have seen remarkable miracles while people walked in supernatural faith to do supernatural things.

All of these activities and movements of the Spirit are gifts. They are given to us for the edification and strengthening of the Church, His people, His Bride. These same gifts are also available to us to walk in the supernatural ways of the kingdom on a daily, regular basis if we will activate them.

Gifts are *received* not earned, but Paul indicates that we can position ourselves to receive as we *"eagerly desire"* the gifts (1 Cor. 12:31 NIV). By the Scripture pattern, the primary way of receiving fresh gifts is as we receive fresh fillings of the Holy Spirit (see Acts 4:31). God has placed within us the third person of the Trinity to commune and to help us on a daily basis. This is one way we get to speak to Him today. This is a how to live from the inside out—truly the best way to live.

HE WILLS

But one and the same Spirit works all these things, distributing to each one individually as He wills (1 Corinthians 12:11).

There has been much confusion surrounding the will of God when it comes to spiritual gifts. The confusing part is the notion that unless God decides to give these gifts we cannot receive them or ask for them. A great deal is made of the Bible text that He will "distribute to each as He wills" (see 1 Cor. 12:11). It is perfectly right that the gifts are in His will, but Paul is not dealing with *whether* He will give them; Paul is dealing with *what He will give* to each individual. It is not so much the withholding as it is the distribution of the gifts that lies within His will in First Corinthians 12.

We are encouraged to desire and ask for spiritual gifts. These are part of our inheritance as sons and daughters of the King. Again, these spiritual gifts are not to be confused with what we can operate in daily through life in the Spirit. After all, we have the Spirit of God living in us.

BAPTISM OF THE HOLY SPIRIT

When the Day of Pentecost had fully come, they were all with one accord in one place. And suddenly there came a sound from heaven, as of a rushing mighty wind, and it filled the whole house where they were sitting. Then there appeared to them divided tongues, as of fire, and one sat upon each of them. And they were all filled with the Holy Spirit and began to speak with other tongues, as the Spirit gave them utterance (Acts 2:1-4).

So Jesus said to them again, "Peace to you! As the Father has sent Me, I also send you." And when He had said this, He breathed on them, and said to them, "Receive the Holy Spirit." (John 20:21-22).

Like all of God's gifts, *we receive the baptism of the Holy Spirit by faith.* It is a gift of grace—we must simply ask the Lord! With humble hearts, we ask the Holy Spirit who lives within us as believers to fill us and empower us with Himself.

Paul commands us to *"not be drunk with wine...but be filled with the Spirit..."* (Eph. 5:18). In the Greek, it is literally a command to "keep on being filled to the brim with the Spirit." Therefore, though we receive a most definite "baptism in the Holy Spirit," we eagerly desire to be filled over and over in Him throughout our journey in Christlikeness.

> *He who believes in Me, as the Scripture has said, out of his heart will flow rivers of living water* (John 7:38).

What an incredible truth: the Creator of the universe lives and abides inside of me. I speak to Him spirit to Spirit and from within me flow rivers of living water. The very same power that raised Jesus from the dead lives inside of me, and I get to commune with Him daily. That is why I can guarantee, if you want a prayer life full of encounter and filled with real power, ask the Father for an infilling of the Holy Spirit and begin to pray out mysteries, building yourself up, charging yourself, with the power of God.

What an awesome reality. God Himself lives in us and rivers of living water will flow out of us. I pray this reality would mark you forever!

THE CHALLENGE

If you currently pray in tongues, don't look at it as a badge of honor to be worn and not used. If a fire is left unattended, it will burn lower and lower and will eventually go out. It becomes ineffective in fueling its purpose (heating). I challenge you to increase your time in praying in tongues. I suggest making this a daily part of your prayer life. If you pray in tongues for ten minutes, increase your time to thirty minutes; and if you pray in tongues for thirty minutes, increase your time to an hour a day. If you pray in tongues one hour, increase to two or three.

Not long ago, a young man named Caleb was with me in my car. He had recently given his life to the Lord at our Pursuit Internship. Caleb had a powerful encounter with God; He was freed from drugs, oppression, and much sin. He was also water baptized and filled with the Spirit, all in the same week.

This particular day, Caleb went with me and my two sons, Michael and Gabriel, to run some errands. I asked him about his time praying in tongues and how it had affected him. I was expecting to hear similar encounters to my own. To my disappointment, Caleb had not found praying in tongues all that supernatural. He proceeded to tell me that he believed in it because it's in the Bible. But, although he already had begun using his prayer language, he had not felt anything when he prayed. He was beginning to question whether or not it had real power. I asked him how long he prayed in tongues and he told me about five to ten minutes.

Although it's not necessarily about the number of minutes a person prays in tongues, it does take time to progress from mostly thinking about yourself, to focusing your attention on the God who resides inside of you. Communing with Him, spirit to Spirit, takes time.

We had twenty minutes in the car to reach our destination, so I encouraged Caleb to pray in tongues with me for the full twenty minutes. I said to him, "All right, let's pray in tongues for the next twenty minutes straight. Let's go for it, and you tell me when we reach our destination whether you felt anything."

The four of us *went for it* as I cranked the worship music up. We engaged our spirits and prayed in tongues to God. The presence of God became very thick in the car. As we neared our arrival, I looked back in the rearview mirror, where Caleb was sitting. He was weeping before the Lord; God had obviously touched him deeply.

I tell you this story for you to be encouraged and not give up. Though you might feel the wind of the Holy Spirit sometimes, and sometimes not, the power of God is flowing and you are edifying and recharging your battery as you plug into this supernatural power source.

INVITATION

If you then, being evil, know how to give good gifts to your children, how much more will your heavenly Father give the Holy Spirit to those who ask Him! (Luke 11:13).

For those of you who desire to pray in your prayer language and have yet to experience it, I want to invite you to posture your heart in receiving from God all that He has for you. You can do this right *now*, no need to wait. Simply focus your attention on the Holy Spirit within you and ask Him to fill you. As you wait on Him, when words or syllables begin to come to you, just say them, out loud, while focusing on the throne of God or the Holy Spirit within you. Remember, that all it takes is faith and childlikeness. You may feel silly at first, but soon you will begin to feel the power of this supernatural language. You do have to speak; this is your part in cooperating with the Holy Spirit. Let me explain it better by telling you a story.

My wife was recently in San Diego visiting her sister, and she began talking with one of her sister's friends. The topic of praying in tongues came up. This young woman wanted all she could have in God and asked how to do it. They sat in a vehicle late that night and just simply asked the Holy Spirit to come and fill her.

As they waited, nothing seemed to be happening. One amazing trait of this young woman was her simple faith and childlikeness. She was eager and ready, yet there seemed to be no results. After some time, my wife told her she was confident that words would come to her mind. She told her that, when they did, she should just say them.

They all went home and this young woman called early the next morning. Excitedly she said, "It happened just the way you said it would, a language I have never heard just began to bubble out of me!"

She was so excited and overwhelmed at God's goodness. It was her simple faith that became the avenue for her to receive. She believed it and received it!

Though not every experience is that dramatic, it simply involves a posture of receiving. Why not take the plunge? Invite the Holy Spirit to fill you to overflowing, saturating you with His presence. Receive by faith the gift of tongues and then spend time every day praying in your supernatural prayer language. Pray, pray, pray!

Chapter 12

FASTED LIFESTYLE

*If you say "I will fast when God lays it on my
heart," you never will. You are too cold and
indifferent to take the yoke upon you.*
—D.L. MOODY

CHRISTELLE AND I entered through the doors of the International
House of Prayer in Kansas City (IHOP-KC) in June, 2008. I
was so weak coming straight from the emergency room, that I could
barely walk. I was very sick, but I wanted to encounter God. I didn't
know it then, but walking into the 24-hour House of Prayer that
day would be the beginning of a life-transforming process that would
affect many areas of my life, ministry, and home.

Up until this point of my life, I was a ministry leader directing
evangelistic campaigns and traveling all over the world. Despite some
success in ministry, I had grown cold to the things of God. I had no
prayer life, no Word life, and no intimacy with God. My dead relationship with God affected everything in my life. I did great things
for God, but my life was void of Him in so many ways.

My marriage was a business partnership more than a relationship built in intimacy. We had a relationship that walked side by side, rather than face to face. We came together to discuss the issues of the day, week, or month— the needs of our family in finances, school, sports, or schedules. A real and true heart connection was nowhere in sight. God needed to do something, and fast.

Walking into the 24-hour House of Prayer that day would prove to be a life-altering experience. I was desperate for a fresh touch from Him. My life up to that point was not the vibrant life with God, my wife, and my children that I had pictured as a young boy. Maybe those were fairy tales, but I still had to believe my life could be different with all that God had already given me.

Christelle and I sat together in the prayer room. Both of us had our journals; she had her Bible. We began to worship and pray, and I saw Christelle writing down things God was telling her. I felt so distant and far from God. What did I need to do? Underneath my breath, I cried out to God, "God, I need Your help! Speak to me!"

The moderator of the meeting started inviting people who were physically sick in their bodies to stand up. I didn't like that kind of thing, but Christelle nudged me. I shook my head, "No!"

The speaker continued to invite those who were sick to stand up so that people could pray for them. I hesitantly stood up. A group of people surrounded me and began to pray for my body. After a few minutes of praying over me, people started to leave, then a man started to prophesy over me. His voice became very intense and direct. He said, "You're going to walk a clear, bold, and honest walk, in the spirit of Joel chapter two!" Christelle immediately wrote the words in her journal.

To be honest, I was shocked by those words. I wasn't living that type of lifestyle. Everything in my life was hazy and gray. It was not clear at all. Entertainment had taken a strong hold on my life, to the point that I had to fall asleep watching a movie or a television show.

I could not have any quietness in my life. I would fill my time with every form of entertainment, as much as possible. I would watch any kind of movie and listen to any kind of music.

I had absolutely no boldness in my life at all. I was not standing up for anything that I knew was right. I was weak in every area of my life. I would not speak the Word with boldness and authority because I knew the type of life I had been living.

Shame had such a grip in my life. I had believed the lie that I shouldn't speak or stand up because of how I really walked and how I was spending my time in secret. After all, we must walk the walk and not just talk the talk.

Truth is one of the greatest standards that we have. I was not walking in honesty and integrity at all. Although I started off with sincerity, everything in my life at that point was a facade. You could look at me from the outside and say, there is a good Christian leader doing great things. But in reality, my life was weak and feeble, powerless with no substance.

It all came from the lack of God in my life.

SHOCKED

The prophetic word from that gentleman was fine and dandy up until that point. It had not taken any real effect in my life yet. I just thought it was a guy talking some nonsense, really. Two hours later however, I was in for the shock of my life. Christelle and I had an appointment in the prophetic rooms at IHOP-KC. This is where two or three people from the ministry team prophesy over you and ask for some thoughts from the Lord for your life.

We entered the room, sat down with a few people who were going to pray over us and tell us what was on God's heart. After a couple minutes of explanation and introduction, they began to pray into a recording device. The young man sitting in front of us began to prophesy. "God is calling you to walk a clear, bold, and honest walk, in the spirit of Joel chapter two."

I sat there stunned by the exact words spoken by the guy who prayed over me earlier. *Was this the same guy?* I wondered. No, he wasn't. Was God trying to get my attention? Yes, He was! And He had it. As soon as we were done praying, I ran next door and bought a Bible and looked up Joel 2. I had never read the Book of Joel and if I had, it had no impact on my life prior to that day.

Please read these words carefully. I believe these are the words with which God is calling this generation!

> *"Now, therefore," says the LORD, "Turn to Me with all your heart, with fasting, with weeping, and with mourning." So rend your heart, and not your garments; return to the LORD your God, for He is gracious and merciful, slow to anger, and of great kindness; and He relents from doing harm. Who knows if He will turn and relent, and leave a blessing behind Him—a grain offering and a drink offering for the LORD your God? Blow the trumpet in Zion, consecrate a fast, call a sacred assembly; gather the people, sanctify the congregation, assemble the elders, gather the children and nursing babes; let the bridegroom go out from his chamber, and the bride from her dressing room. Let the priests, who minister to the LORD, weep between the porch and the altar; let them say, "Spare Your people, O LORD, and do not give Your heritage to reproach, that the nations should rule over them. Why should they say among the peoples, 'Where is their God?'"* (Joel 2:12-17).

God was calling me to a rendering of my heart and therefore a transformation of my life. He was calling me to a lifestyle of prayer, fasting, and complete surrender. He was restoring the first commandment to love Him with all my heart, soul, and strength. Unbeknownst to me, fasting was going to be the catalyst to render my heart to the Lord.

In contrast, I had been dependent on doing things in my own strength, in ministry and throughout my life. I came to a point that it seemed I really did not need God. Then suddenly, the bankruptcy in my life became my new reality, and I realized I could not do this on my own anymore.

In my pursuit of holiness, it was always my trying to strive in my strength to make vows and commitments that I would do this or that or not do this sin or that one; but eventually I would fall short. I wanted true freedom in every area of my life. I also wanted God to take over my public ministry life, so that I could speak with anointing and boldness that was not my own. I wanted my ministry to come from a heart that was clean and pure. I didn't want a mediocre, status-quo ministry life anymore. I wanted true heart change and I was desperate to get it.

I deeply loved my wife and wanted what we set out to accomplish on our wedding day: a lifelong relationship that would grow into a fulfilled life for one another. God had blessed me with an extraordinary gift and I wanted to take hold of the fullness of this amazing covenant with one another. Consequently, I knew there was great intimacy that we could share that went beyond the marriage bed. I asked God to give it to me!

I know that my kids watch me intently, learning and studying my every word and action. Prior to this, the example I had given them showed a separation of my true life and God. What I did in public was way different from what I did behind closed doors. Looking back now, my home was a home of entertainment, not a home of prayer.

God was calling for a full life change in every area! I was ecstatic to finally begin taking my life and home in the direction I had really always wanted.

FASTING

I want to focus the rest of the chapter on a subject that is often misrepresented and oftentimes looked at as optional in the Christian walk: *fasting*. I want to talk on this subject because it was key for me in my heart transformation process. This powerful tool became not only an accelerator in God, but brought much freedom from demonic influence and sin in my life.

The power to accomplish remarkable feats and live an exceptional life is not tied to an occupation, a personality, or a network, but to a disposition of the heart, which comes from living a fasted lifestyle. God was after my heart, not my occupation or what I could offer Him.

Fasting is that propeller that rends the heart like nothing in life can ever do. If you want a life change and are not satisfied with your spiritual walk, your prayer life, your marriage, or anything else, look no further than one of the greatest tools for success: a lifestyle of fasting!

I believe God is calling this generation to live a fasted lifestyle. So let's look at what fasting is and how we can implement it in our lives.

WHAT IS FASTING?

As I stated in an earlier chapter, there are many misconceptions about fasting. Fasting is not merely going without food for a period of time. It is not about starving yourself; nor is fasting done by only the radicals or fanatics. The practice of fasting is not limited to ministers or to special occasions.

Biblical fasting is refraining from food for a spiritual purpose. When you eliminate food from your diet for a number of days, your spirit becomes realigned and sensitive to the things of God. It is essentially focusing on feeding your spirit and denying your flesh for a greater pleasure.

The Sermon on the Mount, found in Matthew, provides a pattern by which each of us is to live. The pattern addresses three commitments to live by. Jesus said, *"When you give…"* and *"when you pray…"* and *"when you fast."* He made it clear that fasting (like giving and praying), is a normal part of the Christian life. Better said, it *should be* a normal part of our Christian walk.

I would suggest that it is not possible to live biblical Christianity without being committed to a lifestyle of prayer, fasting, giving, serving, and blessing our enemies. Christianity void of these five elements is not New Testament Christianity. We are called to live a fasted lifestyle. Obviously there are exceptions for those who have health problems or are pregnant. If you can't fast from eating food there are many other ways you are able to fast.

BESETTING SINS

I had done small fasts in the past. In 2000, I successfully completed a 21-day water fast. It was a great time with the Lord. It was also a great time with a friend who joined me in fasting, with times of prayer.

In June 2008, I entered into a seven-day fast without the intent or focus on breaking things in my life. However, God used this time of fasting to immediately break off various appetites that I had lived with for too long.

> *Therefore we also, since we are surrounded by so great a cloud of witnesses, let us lay aside every weight, and the sin which so easily ensnares us, and let us run with endurance the race that is set before us.* (Hebrews 12:1).

Fasting is not only an aid in deliverance from addictions and physical appetites, but God also gives us this grace for the pulling down of demonic strongholds in our minds. God wants us free from *besetting sins* and the lies about our identity that entrap us.

I love this explanation on besetting sins from the book, *The Rewards of Fasting,* by Mike Bickle and Dana Candle:

> Besetting sins are more serious than sins into which we stumble on occasion. They are habitual actions or attitudes that hold God's people in bondage....Common sins that beset people in bondage include pornography, immorality, anger, drugs, tobacco, and different eating disorders.... Isaiah exhorts us to fast to "loose the bonds of wickedness" (Is. 58:6), that we might be freed from the sinful behavior to which we are addicted....Willpower is not strong enough to break us free of besetting sins. Strongholds are demonically energized; they are established on territory Satan has been given rights to hold, either through our sin or the sin of those in the generations before us.[1]

"Regardless of how we are involved, we must ruthlessly repent of all that we've done to allow spiritual strongholds"[2] to be established in our lives. We must not neglect the power that fasting and prayer have in breaking off addictions and demolishing strongholds.

LIFESTYLE FASTS

In *7 Commitments of a Forerunner,* Mike Bickle offers a range of fasting methods:

> I suggest five different fasts that we may participate in.
>
> The first is a *regular fast*, which entails going without food and drinking only water, or liquid that has very little or no calories.
>
> The second is a *liquid fast*, which is going without solid food and drinking only light liquids, such as fruit and vegetable juices.

Third, the *partial fast*, includes abstaining from tasty foods and eating only vegetables or nuts. This was the fast chosen by Daniel, who ate only vegetables and drank only water (Dan. 1:12).

Fourth, the *Benedict fast* was established by Saint Benedict and consisted of eating only one meal a day.

Lastly, the *absolute fast*, or Esther fast, includes abstaining from food and water. This fast should only be participated in with extreme caution, as going without water should never be done for more than one to three days.[3]

The level at which a person engages in fasting from food should be determined according to age and with regard to any physical illness....Those with a known or suspected physical disability or illness, or with any history of an eating disorder, should never fast except in consultation with, and under the supervision of a qualified physician. Children are also discouraged from fasting food and should never engage in a fast without express parental consent and oversight. Minors who desire to fast should consider a Daniel fast or non-food abstentions, such as: TV, movies, Internet surfing, video games, and other forms of entertainment. The Bible does not call children to fast.[4]

When we become jealous for impact on our spirit, living out the fasted lifestyle is essential to position ourselves to receive more freely from God.[5]

As you embark on this lifestyle of prayer and fasting, God will give you the grace for fasting.

In living a lifestyle of fasting I am convinced that you will see the benefits of living this out on a regular basis. Anytime we forego earthly pleasures to gain more heavenly ones we reap great rewards. These rewards are felt even here during our time on earth.

Chapter 13

MORAVIAN PASSION

The closest thing to the New Jerusalem
that could be found on the earth. I would
gladly have spent my life there.
—JOHN WESLEY

A FULL GENERATION BEFORE the modern missions movement began under the inspiration of William Carey; a small group of three hundred young radicals dedicated themselves to carrying out the Great Commission.

Sent from Europe to the farthest reaches of the globe, these young men and women didn't need the usual titles and prestige of clergy. In fact, they would gladly sell themselves into slavery, simply to reach those who had not heard the name of Jesus and all for one purpose—that "the lamb, who was slain, would receive the reward of His suffering."

Count Nikolaus von Zinzendorf was born into a wealthy aristocratic family. Historians call him "the rich young ruler who said yes."[1] In his book, *Three Witnesses: John Hus, Jon Amos Comenius, and*

Count Nikolaus Ludwig von Zinzendorf, Rick Joyner says Zinzendorf was "destined to sit on one of the continent's most powerful thrones; yet he gave it all up and spent his life and fortune to carry the gospel to the ends of the earth."[2] This one man's zeal for the Lord so transformed modern Christianity that it would be impossible to measure the full impact of his life on the Church or the world. "If Luther had changed the Church by standing for truth, Zinzendorf changed it by standing for love."[3] When Zinzendorf was twenty-seven years old, he took into his estate a single Moravian refugee. Before long, Zinzendorf had three hundred Moravian refugees living on his estate and he became their spiritual leader. They all lived in a village called Hernnhut, in Germany. "This was the name of Zinzendorf's estate and meant 'under the Lord's watch.'"[4] Count Zinzendorf sparked a spiritual revolution that was profoundly different from anything history had ever seen. As Zinzendorf was studying the history of these Moravian people, "he came across a document that talked about John Amos Comenius' 100-year prophecy."[5] In this document John Amos "had prophesied that 100 years later a revival would sprout forth from this hidden seed."[6] Zinzendorf realized that it was exactly 100 years almost to the day; a new resolve was ignited within him. Zinzendorf brought a group together for an entire night of prayer and reading the Book of John. Many of them did not sleep as they were anticipating God was going to do something significant.

"Wednesday, August 13, 1727 is referred to in history as "the Moravian Pentecost."[7] The Holy Spirit came down upon the Moravians in a powerful way. One Moravian gave testimony: "We discovered therein the finger of God, and found ourselves, as it were, baptized under the cloud of our fathers, with their spirit. For the Spirit came again upon us, and great signs and wonders were wrought among the brethren in those days, and great grace prevailed among us, and in the whole country."[8] This became such an extraordinary place that even John Wesley would go on to say that Herrnhut "might be the closest thing to the New Jerusalem that could be found on the earth but he also added "I would gladly have spent my life there."[9] The immediate result of the outpouring was the start of a prayer vigil. At any given hour, three people were praying together in the place of prayer. This prayer meeting would last over one hundred years. This is truly unbelievable! A prayer meeting that went on day and night, never stopping, for over a century! The Moravians fell in love with God. They spent hours in prayer because they understood the reality that this is how they could make real impactful change. They were fueled by the power of the Holy Spirit. The Moravians had a passion that inspired them to leave their homes and comforts to tell the world of this great love.

The Moravians began to burn for the unreached peoples of the world—people who had never heard about Jesus Christ. What is remarkable is that out of this prayer meeting the Moravian Missions Movement and the Methodist Revival would be birthed. This small group of three hundred Moravians sent out missionaries to live among unreached peoples all over the world, learning their language and culture, and telling them about Jesus Christ.

What is more astonishing about the Moravian missionaries, is that there were some who even voluntarily sold themselves into slavery so that they could identify with slaves and share the gospel with them.

INCENSE RISING

"From the rising of the sun, even to its going down, my name shall be great among the Gentiles; in every place incense shall be offered to My name, and a pure offering; for My name shall be great among the nations," says the LORD of hosts (Malachi 1:11).

A global worship and prayer movement is currently rising in many places all over the earth. There is a rediscovering of the character of

God. Prayer and music are coming together. God is orchestrating a worship and prayer phenomenon on the earth in our generation. The Body of Christ is becoming *"a house of prayer for all nations"* (Isa. 56:7) and millions are coming to Christ. Prayer has been emerging and worship is ushering in His presence like never before in human history. He is worth all the affections of all the saints. Unceasing 24/7 adoration is happening all over the world. It's rising right now. I believe this prayer and worship movement will usher in the great outpouring of His Spirit, and I believe He is preparing our hearts and lives for that very moment.

A dying world does not need our fancy buildings and programs, even though buildings serve a purpose. What the world really needs to experience is a life-altering encounter where people are marked by the glory of His presence resting among them! We have an incredible privilege to host Him, the One who heals the heartaches, and much more in our midst!

TIME TO BUILD THE HOUSE OF PRAYER

November 1, 2008 was a significant day for our family and ministry. Everything changed for us.

My wife and I were alone on this particular weekend in Toronto, Ontario, where I was finishing facilitating a gathering of leaders from across Canada. Our children were not with us. I was busy with meetings throughout the day. At around 5:00 A.M., I was awakened from a sound sleep.

I seem to get awakened a lot. It is probably the best way for God to get my attention! I heard the Lord's voice. To this day, I can't tell you if it was an audible voice outside of my body or the internal voice of God, but what I can tell you is that it echoed inside my body for at least sixty seconds. I was frozen, not knowing how to respond or what to say.

I heard the following words repeated over and over again; *"You just conceived a boy. His name is Justice. Now is the time to build the house of prayer."* As these words ignited my heart, I began to get really excited. I didn't know whether to cry or to laugh. Then it hit me; I'm having a baby boy! I also knew his name. How awesome is that? We already had three boys at this time, and one girl. My siblings and my extended family also have a lot of boys, and boys' names had been somewhat of a challenge for us. Not this time; we knew his name already. His name was *Justice*.

I then considered the words, *Now is the time to build the house of prayer.* I didn't know what that really meant or what to do about it. I immediately awakened Christelle and told her what I heard. We didn't say much; we just had a sobering, yet excited feeling in us. I led Christelle to kneel down next to the bed. We proceeded to thank God for the baby boy that we were going to have and we didn't know what "building a house of prayer" really meant, so we agreed to simply say yes to Him. "Whatever it looks like, whatever it takes, we will build the house of prayer," we agreed.

At this point we had already been praying regularly and faithfully. Our house and family had transformed into a literal house of prayer where our family time was no longer scheduled around a movie or some sort of entertainment, but around a prayer meeting. Following this encounter, we delved into the Word and began to pray out Scripture. We began to pray in the Spirit and much more. Our kids were encountering God on a regular basis and growing spiritually right in front of our eyes.

On a corporate level, coming from a purely evangelistic background, we still had no idea of how to build a house of prayer. Nor did we know what it would look like. We began to learn and study about prayer and worship, and God led us every step of the way!

GLOBAL PRAYER HOUSE

From the day that we said yes to the Lord to build Global Prayer House (GPH), we really had no idea of the work and effort it entailed. Not only was it physical work, but also the process was testing my resolve, revealing my heart, and building my character. You see, up until this point I had been involved in large campaign-style evangelism with Impact World Tour, a ministry of YWAM. We had traveled the world, moving every three to six months. I had seen huge crowds turn out to our events, and witnessed large numbers of salvations and rededications to the Lord. I also enjoyed the prestige and the notoriety that this brought. The Global Prayer House in itself was a testing of my character and how I would respond to the lack of praise from men.

I always thought of myself as an evangelist, but now my heart was expanding even more. What began to grow in the heart of Christelle and me and I was not only a burning to know God, but an urge to awaken the sleeping giant, the Church, to what life is all about. This urge was growing to include so much more than reaching the lost; it was also about reigniting the hearts of the lost within the walls of the Church. It was about those who, just like us, were so busy "doing" that they had lost the reason why we are here, which is intimacy with Him.

This deep desire within me to raise up a place filled with His presence on the earth grew and drove me. I can't adequately describe what I felt, other than I knew *I had to do this.* The Spirit of Awakening (see Joel 2), the desire to build a resting place for the Lord (see Ps. 132), raising up a house of prayer for the nations (see Isa. 56:7), and wanting to gaze on His beauty (see Ps. 27:4), continued to be the fuel in the fire for the journey of building Global Prayer House. These verses among others confirmed time and again that God was distinctly calling us to this task.

We began preparations the first year after God placed the vision for Global Prayer House in my heart. Prior to this, we had thought it might be about our lives and family. Our home had become a miniature house of prayer and our lifestyle choices were already beginning to bear great fruit. Even though we had seen radical heart and behavior changes in our home life, we did not feel ready or equipped to take others into this on a corporate level.

After all, my expertise was evangelism and setting up crusades. I had no idea how to get people to pray or how to raise up singers and musicians. I knew that God wanted me to establish a place of His presence, where God was ministered to and people were refreshed and awakened. I knew that I was to call people to pray and seek His face. Yet the stark contrast of my previous mindset to prayer was ever before me.

It had not been long ago that I was the guy who hated prayer meetings and worship services. I thought that I was doing the "real" work and intercessors were wasting their time hiding away in a room praying. I began to realize that the very people God was asking me to reach out to, were the people who were just like I was: those that were sincere or had started out well, but did not have a heart connection with the lover of their souls.

This task, though daunting, began to brew in me an excitement of what could be possible when the Church became awakened to the fact that they are the Bride. What could happen with an army of not only workers, but lovers of God? I felt the favor of God on my life in a very real and tangible way. The vision that began to be birthed in my heart was one of personal revival, corporate awakening, and a worldwide sweep of souls coming to Christ. I could see before me the rough, ugly, disgruntled and in-debt believers, like I was. They were all around me, and I began to see them as the mighty men and women of God, just like David's mighty men.

The first months after we made the decision to put legs to this vision, we decided to have a prayer meeting. We invited everyone we knew in the area, and about seventy-five people showed up. We had a friend lead worship and we prayed out apostolic prayers over the region.

It was wonderful! The Holy Spirit was evident, people were being touched, and God was being exalted. We left that meeting feeling encouraged, fueled up, and ready to go. However, what followed was far from easy and successful in the eyes of man. We went from having monthly prayer to weekly prayer. We had a couple of worship leaders who loved Jesus come and lead and Christelle and I prayed into the microphone. These weekly meetings started out strong, but in a few weeks they had dwindled to an average of seven people in the room—Christelle and I, the worship leader, the sound guy and his wife, and two good friends of ours. Occasionally we would bring our kids and have eleven people! At first this was OK, but over time we began to question whether we really had heard God. After all, wouldn't we see more fruit already?

This certainly was not the success we had pictured. According to man's measurement, this was a far cry from any of our previous meetings while working in evangelistic campaigns. There were no crowds, a small room with very little heat in the winter (sometimes no heat), and seven people. No one even knew we were there. Not only that, but we had very little finances for ministry and we were living in a city and a country where we had no family anywhere near us. The questions began to flood me: Was this really God? Maybe I was wrong? This, however, was exactly where God wanted me.

Over the next year we had a choice to make; would we dig in our heels and trust that God had really spoken, or would we quit and move back to the United States? It was a real time of testing. On top of this, I was offered several well-paying jobs with prestigious positions. Each time I said no, however, I wondered if I was making a grave mistake.

Doubt was creeping in. In the midst of this process, we postponed prayer for awhile and went down to the States to visit family. On this trip we really prayed and asked God to confirm again that this was Him. While on our trip I cannot really explain it, except to say that Christelle and I both began to have a sick feeling that we were in great disobedience to God by even stopping the prayer for a season.

We immediately knew that the house of prayer was not our idea, but an idea birthed from the heart of God. We got on our knees, and repented before God. When we went home we never looked back.

Needless to say, this was not easy; we had many challenges along the way. God was faithful though, providing each thing as we needed it, yet with the tension of holding back enough to keep us reaching and asking. No longer though, did I care about the numbers or what success we appeared to have or not have. I knew that God saw and was delighted with my heart of obedience and willingness to give my whole life to this cause. I knew that pleasing and obeying Him was true success.

God even began to provide key friendships, relationships, and staff. He brought us two wonderful couples to be full-time staff in the very early days. These people saw the vision and poured their lives and hearts out for something that did not even exist yet.

As time went on, God brought us exactly the right people we needed, at the right times. He continues to do this. As I am writing this, I can say that we have the best team we could ever have. They are not only excellent in skill, but they are first and foremost passionate lovers of Jesus. I thank God for each team member and the friendships He brought to us at such key moments in the journey.

I cannot even begin to give you the whole picture of what God has taken us through in our hearts since starting Global Prayer House and the Pursuit movement, including conferences, internships, and home groups. I know it is only the beginning of a great journey with the Lord. God has always been more concerned about having us for

Himself and having our entire heart than any other thing. I count it a privilege and an honor to even be used of God. This is my prayer:

> *Lord, I want all of You that I can possibly have. Whatever else happens and whatever ministry call You ask of me, I am willing. But may You always have my heart. And may I never lose sight ever again of my first call; to love You with all my heart, mind, soul, and strength.*

UNDERSTANDING PRAYER

We were created to interact deeply with God's heart. God speaks and it moves our hearts. We speak and it moves God's heart. The result is that God's resources are released into the earthly realm. His resources include wisdom (creative ideas), unity, money, impact, zeal for righteousness, etc.

Many people's approach to prayer in terms of intercession is mostly about *revival and power!* Yes, it is about releasing revival and power in many things in terms of God's purposes, but intercession must be connected and energized by encountering God, the Person. If this were not the case in my life, I don't think I would last long in prayer. I can only ask for revival for so long. I want to connect with my eternal, uncreated God as well as declare in intercession the need for revival. More than anything though, I want to speak to God and hear from Him.

INTIMACY, JOY, AND IDENTITY

> *Even them I will bring to My holy mountain, and make them joyful in My house of prayer...for my house shall be called a house of prayer for all nations* (Isaiah 56:7).

God is bringing enjoyable prayer for all nations. This includes intimacy, enjoyment, and identity. God is looking for continual worship and prayer, where His presence can rest. *"The fire on the altar shall be kept burning on it; it shall not be put out..."* (Lev. 6:12).

Our identity as the Church is a House of Prayer. This is what He calls us and this is how He sees us. Our identity as sons of God and the Bride of Christ come together in being His Family or House. The Father has ordained that His family rule with Jesus through intimacy-based intercession. The ultimate purpose of the House of Prayer is to overflow into the nations of the earth (see Isa. 56:7).

God is raising up a worship and prayer movement all over the earth in our generation in the spirit of the tabernacle of David. What does that mean? God is releasing an intense hunger that makes us drop everything and run to meet with Him. Once we encounter the living God face to face and hear the sound of His voice, it will keep us coming back for more.

We often pray the Lord's Prayer found in Matthew 6:10: *"Your kingdom come. Your will be done on earth as it is in heaven."* So before we continue with what the Lord is doing on the earth today and what He's done throughout history, I want to show you this present heavenly reality. I would like to show you the worship that is happening in heaven right now as you read this.

HEAVENLY WORSHIP

Stephen Venable from his teaching *Foundations of Night and Day Worship and Prayer* helps gives great insight into the unveiling of worship and prayer in heaven. Let's journey together as we see this majestic present-day reality.

"Worship, of course, is not an abstract 'atmosphere'— it requires participants. When we think about worship it must evoke a flood of thoughts about a person, not opinions about an activity from which we get something."[10] "By turning our eyes to heaven we are reminded that at the heart of worship lies a consuming preoccupation with

God Himself. We read of myriads of angels tirelessly lauding the glorious King enthroned on high and we are rescued from the self-compulsion that threatens to undermine true worship."[11] By seeing how angels are clearly presented in a role of worship in heaven, our perspective on what transpires inside the heavenly sanctuary will be greatly changed.

Being aware of the reality of heavenly focused worship changes everything. It reveals to us that we are a part of something much more than what we see with our eyes. This is also true of prayer and personal devotion. Stephen Venable goes on to say:

> Personal or corporate devotion will simply never ascend beyond the knowledge of the Person to whom we are devoted. Where the vision of that Person is dim, obscure, or marginalized, true adoration will be rare and fervent cries of intercession scarce. Yet where Christ is treasured and exalted in the hearts of the people, worship and prayer alike will have both their impetus and their staying power. And nowhere are we reminded of this central place theology must hold in incessant devotion as in the heights of heaven where God Himself is all in all.[12]

What is happening right now is truly remarkable. First, let me begin by describing the three heavens. This is not exhaustive by any means but will hopefully give us an idea of the bigger picture.

THE FIRST HEAVEN

Biblically, the first heaven is what we understand to be the sky and the atmosphere, that which is visible to our eyes. In the beginning God created the waters (see Gen 1:1-8; 2 Pet. 3:5), and then divided them in a vast circular shape.

Praise Him, you heavens of heavens, and you waters above the heavens! (Psalm 148:4).

It is He who sits above the circle of the earth, and its inhabitants are like grasshoppers, who stretches out the heavens like a curtain and spreads them out like a tent to dwell in (Isaiah 40:22).

THE SECOND HEAVEN

The mid-heavens can be understood, not as the dwelling place of God, but as the domain of angels, the place of delegated authority, where both good and evil purposes for the earth are contended. Understanding this is so significant to our worship and prayer life. When we are asking God in intercession to release something, a great battle is forged in the second heaven and our prayers hold great weight with repercussions here on earth.

For we do not wrestle against flesh and blood, but against principalities, against powers, against the rulers of the darkness of this age, against spiritual hosts of wickedness in the heavenly places (Ephesians 6:12).

Although the mid-heavens are the least defined by Scripture, they are still presented in profoundly concrete terms. The angel Gabriel was said to *"fly swiftly"* in Daniel 9:21 from one location to another. Then in Daniel 10:13 he was physically detained by the prince of Persia.

Then he said to me, "Do not fear, Daniel, for from the first day that you set your heart to understand, and to humble yourself before your God, your words were heard; and I have come because of your words. But the prince of the kingdom of Persia withstood me twenty-one days; and behold, Michael, one of the chief princes, came to help me, for I had been left alone there with the kings of

Persia. Now I have come to make you understand what will happen to your people in the latter days, for the vision refers to many days yet to come" (Daniel 10:12-14).

THE THIRD HEAVEN

The third heaven is the place we dream about and there are a lot of fairy tale ideas of what this place really looks like. The study of heaven gives me a new reality and it also gives me a desire and a longing to be there. As I study and learn about heaven, I have to tell you, I can't wait to go home!

Paul wrote in Second Corinthians 12:1-4:

It is doubtless not profitable for me to boast. I will come to visions and revelations of the Lord: I know a man in Christ who fourteen years ago— whether in the body I do not know, or whether out of the body I do not know, God knows—such a one was caught up to the third heaven. And I know such a man—whether in the body or out of the body I do not know, God knows—how he was caught up into Paradise and heard inexpressible words, which it is not lawful for a man to utter.

The third heaven is first, the dwelling place of God. Jesus refers to His Father being "in heaven" fourteen times in Matthew alone. Jesus descends from heaven and is described as ascending to heaven and being exalted at the right hand of the throne of God in heaven. Jesus will come from heaven when He returns.

The LORD looks from heaven; He sees all the sons of men (Psalm 33:13).

Second, the third heaven is the everlasting home of the redeemed. This is where we are making treasures (see Matt. 6:20). Our reward is in heaven (see 1 Pet. 1:4) and our citizenship is in heaven (see Phil. 3:20).

The incense of our prayers rise *before God* as He sits on His throne. When the Body of Christ unites in a city to offer Jesus unceasing devotion, there is actually more incense that rises before Him as He is enthroned in His temple. If we actually believed this it would change everything. Oh, for a revelation of the privilege and power of prayer!

> Prayer, like worship, is personally oriented. We are praying to a Person and our intercession is oriented around a real location. Jesus has an authentic human body and He is in an actual place in heaven. In intercession we are approaching the supreme Governor in the governmental center of the universe. That is why through faith we "come before" the throne of God (see Eph. 3, Heb. 4). All intercession is oriented around a real throne in a governmental context. Prayer is not hurling phrases into the air and hoping they are heard in some abstract way. We are making requests that are being considered in a real place, by a real Person: the sovereign King of all things.[13]

Right now the Lord is on His throne and His kingdom rules over all. God reigns over all things, He upholds all things, He sustains all things, and He possesses all things.

There is a dramatic picture of the vast scale of angelic worship that is strikingly recorded in two passages from Revelation:

> *Then I looked, and I heard the voice of many angels around the throne, the living creatures, and the elders; and the number of them was ten thousand times ten thousand, and thousands of thousands, saying with a loud voice; "Worthy is the Lamb who was slain to receive power*

and riches and wisdom, and strength and honor and glory and blessing!" (Revelation 5:11-12).

All the angels stood around the throne and the elders and the four living creatures, and fell on their faces before the throne and worshiped God, saying: "Amen! Blessing and glory and wisdom, thanksgiving and honor and power and might, be to our God forever and ever. Amen" (Revelation 7:11-12).

"This gives us a glimpse of the angelic hosts as they minister in God's temple in heaven who sing to Him and give Him praise. This worship is 'continual,' occurring 'always,' never ceasing even through the night."[14] The angels are divided into various ranks and classes and the position in the hierarchy in some cases dictates their role in the worship of heaven. There is a fully developed structure in the heavenly temple in which the angels participate and lead.

OUR MAKER AND DESIGN

God enjoys music; we are made in His image, and so we have the capacity to enjoy and make music. Zephaniah 3:17 describes how God sings over us: *"The Lord your God in your midst, the Mighty One, will save; He will rejoice over you with gladness, He will quiet you with His love, He will rejoice over you with singing."*

God is a singer. Have you ever thought of God like that? The magnetic "draw" you have to melody is due to the fact that our Maker is the author of music. He creates sounds that you have never heard before. And He sings over you today. He sings over you with gladness. He rejoices over you with singing! What an awesome awareness of God. I believe He even prophetically sings out His intercession over you.

Another massive implication of this truth is that we do not just include music in our worship on earth because it makes it easier or more exciting to worship. We include music because it is integrally woven into the fabric of God's desire and design for worship. "The fact that the Bible so clearly places songs and instruments around the throne of God must not be viewed merely as an interesting fact, but as a theological epiphany that inflicts a blow to our hearts from which we never hope to recover."[15] One of the saddest things for me is knowing that many groups have music in their meetings only as a *warm up* to their gatherings or *entry point* to their talks. Even though this has value, worship is much more than this. It's also much more than just a way to hype someone up to get them to move out of their comfort zone. Music and sound are in our very nature and composition. And worship is the response to the Creator of our frame. Worship is music, sound, emotion, declaration, and responsiveness to our only satisfaction of our souls—God Himself.

ANGELS WORSHIP

I saw the Lord sitting on a throne, high and lifted up, and the train of His robe filled the temple. Above it stood seraphim; each one had six wings: with two he covered his face, with two he covered his feet, and with two he flew. And one cried to another and said: "Holy, holy, holy is the LORD of hosts; the whole earth is full of His glory!" (Isaiah 6:1-3).

Here we see that the seraphim are crying to one another. The burning ones utter declarations of His glory as they hover around the throne of God. One thing we can be sure, by looking at this—worship isn't random. There is a specific order of worship in heaven, and that order has a design. Understanding this gives us confidence to reproduce it on the earth even when we have not yet discovered God's wisdom in ordaining it to the extent we desire.

The driving force for unceasing adoration is very important. The *what* of worship in heaven is vitally important, but even more paramount is the *why* behind the activity that constantly surrounds the throne in the heavenly temple.

> The Seraphim and the larger angelic hosts who are enraptured with ministry to Him have never had a single sin forgiven, never an ailment healed, and never a financial need met and yet their testimony is that His unending glory warrants their unending praise. As they take in the glory of God with all of their eyes, it is so overwhelming and so severe in its magnitude that it necessitates their unbroken adoration. In other words, their ceaseless worship is based solely upon the glory of who He is.[16]

Most of our worship today is often seen primarily through the eyes of man and our need. But worship is so much more glorious. The fact that He is glorious, majestic, and worthy reveals that any of our needs or problems pale in comparison. Worship any other way is lesser than the greatest way to worship Him.

The only purpose for the seraphim to worship is to magnify, extol, and proclaim His surpassing glory. "They are not *changing the atmosphere* in the heavenly temple or doing it so that revival will break out in the Holy City, nor will they have a change in vocation or personal advancement because of their activity."[17] They don't worship because they want a better marriage or better kids or something they lack.

In summary, both the motivation of their sustaining force and aim of unceasing worship is solely His glory. They worship because He is worthy. We still worship in response to His goodness and kindness in our lives, but even if nothing goes right, He's still worthy!

DAVID'S TABERNACLE

David first understood that the Lord longed for hearts that would continually offer worship and praise to God (see Ps. 69:30-31). I believe David saw this heavenly worship (see 1 Chron. 22–23). He was enthralled with this reality in heaven, and felt compelled to build a place of His presence as close to Him as possible. This led David to establish a new order of worship in Israel.

Approximately 1050 B.C., David set up a tent in Jerusalem where night and day worship with singers and musicians took place before the ark of God (presence of God); this was the tabernacle of David. God longed to be continually intimate with His people. He wanted the hearts of His people to continually burn with His very own passion and fire. He longs for this still today.

David's tabernacle continued in ceaseless worship and adoration to the Lord as an answer to God's desire for continual intimacy with His people. Worship in David's tabernacle took place before the ark of the Lord in an open forum where people could come and worship freely.

David's tabernacle used 288 Levites who were gifted in singing the prophetic songs of the Lord (see 1 Chron. 25:7). These singers were broken down into 24-hour teams, each with twelve members (see 1 Chron. 25:9-31) This group of gifted singers led a larger group of 4,000 musicians. They used instruments that David designed himself (see 1 Chron. 23:5). Another 4,000 gatekeepers took care of the service in the tabernacle. Altogether, 8,000 Levites were employed full-time to offer night and day worship and praise before the ark of the Lord. In this environment, David wrote the majority of his psalms.

Six other kings of Judah practiced night and day prayer according to the Davidic order of worship. Each of these kings experienced seasons of blessing and revival in their kingdom. When a king did not keep the Davidic order of worship, the kingdom would begin to lose direction and the people would give themselves to idol worship.

My belief is that when there is no godly night and day worship, people will always worship something. We are designed to worship our Creator, our Father, and out of this love, we worship night and day. Without this, we lose our focus and identity and end up worshiping modern day "idols."

In summary, David, the Moravians and the angels worship the King because He is worthy. God is drawing His people to His house of prayer to inhabit their adoration and attract the unbelievers of the nations. I am forever amazed that we get to join heaven, the Moravians' passion, and David's tabernacle to touch God's heart and overflow in love to people.

Chapter 14

BURN FOR HIM

You never have to advertise a fire. Everyone comes
running when there's a fire. Likewise, if your
church is on fire, you will not have to advertise
it. The community will already know it.
—LEONARD RAVENHILL

*I came to send fire on the earth, and how I wish it were
already kindled! But I have a baptism to be baptized
with, and how distressed I am till it is accomplished!
(Luke 12:49-50).*

YOU WEREN'T MEANT to just barely make it by, struggling with
sin and a life of complacency. You are meant to burn! You are
meant to live a life on fire! Jesus wants to separate the passionate, true,
wholehearted, sincere worship of God, from dead, formal religion. He
does this by sending upon us the fire of the Holy Spirit. His premier
desire is to commune with us at the deepest level possible. Jesus has a
baptism ready to be poured out on you and me. It's a baptism of fire,

of kindling, burning, and passion that will change your life, the lives around you, as well as whole cities and nations. We are in desperate need of this baptism of fire today!

In 2010, I was in the front row of our ministry's annual, Pursuit Conference. During a time of response at the altar, the speaker began to spur the entire room to pray in tongues. I could feel the weightiness of the Holy Spirit's presence increasing on us. I was standing near the front, next to another speaker at the conference and saw him being touched deeply by God.

As I scanned the crowd, I saw people of all walks of life, though seemingly hesitant at first, begin to fervently pray in tongues. As the crowd heightened their intensity, I noticed it was as if *kindling*, or *the starting of a fire* began to crackle in the room. It started out small, but as the roar of tongues increased, it started to feel like a snowball effect in the Spirit.

I can't explain it, except it literally felt like *an open heaven*. As people continued for some time praying in tongues, the speaker then invited the crowd to lay hands on each other, for the baptism of fire. The atmosphere was electric. As soon as everyone started laying hands on one another, the room felt like it erupted. I personally began to be touched deeply with a feeling of heat rising in my heart. This increased in intensity, until it became a trembling fire to my very bones. I was feeling a mixture of conviction, tenderness, and the fear of the Lord.

This wasn't an outward manifestation of the Spirit's power, but an inward burning that felt as if I was on fire from the inside out. It was as if waves of the electricity of His presence, His fire, His awe, His glory, His love, and His majesty were flowing through me and out of me. This manifestation of His presence drew me closer to Him more than I have ever felt. I believe that I was baptized with fire that day and, ever since, I have stayed hungry and postured myself to receive more of this great power in my life. I have tasted fire and I desperately want to be one who continually burns for Him.

WHAT HAPPENS WHEN YOU BURN

When a person gets on fire, everything around him gets hot! Smith Wigglesworth was an uneducated plumber (1859-1947) and was one of the great heroes of faith who moved in extraordinary power and burned from the inside out. He saw multitudes healed with many great signs and wonders that followed him his entire life. He believed that the presence of a man filled with God could bring conviction to sinners without even speaking a word.

One day as Wigglesworth sat opposite of a man in a railway carriage, the man who sat with him suddenly jumped up, exclaimed, "You convict me of sin!" and went into another carriage.

This is one small example of what can happen when a man "burns from the inside out." There are many examples of similar stories in the life of not just Wigglesworth, but in others who lived aflame for Him.

REVIVALIST ON FIRE

Charles Finney is known as a preaching revivalist and a reformer. Finney's mark on history is amazing. He demonstrated that a life is never the same following an encounter with God. There were occasions that the presence of God upon his life changed those around him. Do you want to hear about real fire on a man? Read this excerpt from *Memoirs of Charles G. Finney*!

> There was a cotton manufactory on the Oriskany creek, a little above Whitesboro, a place now called New York Mills. It was owned by a Mr. W, an unconverted man, but a gentleman of high standing and good morals. My brother-in-law, Mr. G A, was at that time superintendent of the factory. I was invited to go and preach at that place, and went up one evening, and preached in the

village schoolhouse, which was large, and was crowded with hearers. The Word, I could see, took powerful effect among the people, especially among the young people who were at work in the factory.

The next morning, after breakfast, I went into the factory, to look through it. As I went through, I observed there was a good deal of agitation among those who were busy at their looms, and their mules, and other implements of work. On passing through one of the apartments, where a great number of young women were attending to their weaving, I observed a couple of them eyeing me, and speaking very earnestly to each other; and I could see that they were a good deal agitated, although they both laughed. I went slowly toward them. They saw me coming, and were evidently much excited. One of them was trying to mend a broken thread, and I observed that her hands trembled so that she could not mend it. I approached slowly, looking on each side at the machinery, as I passed; but observed that this girl grew more and more agitated, and could not proceed with her work. When I came within eight or ten feet of her, I looked solemnly at her. She observed it, and was quite overcome, and sunk down, and burst into tears. The impression caught almost like powder, and in a few moments nearly all in the room were in tears. This feeling spread through the factory. Mr. W, the owner of the establishment, was present and seeing the state of things, he said to the superintendent, "Stop the mill, and let the people attend to religion; for it is more important that our souls should be saved than that this factory run." The gate was immediately shut down, and the factory stopped; but where should we assemble? The superintendent suggested that the mule room was large; and, the mules being run up, we could assemble there. We did so, and a more powerful meeting I scarcely ever attended. It went on with great power. The building was large, and had many people in it, from the garret to the cellar. The revival went through the mill with astonishing power, and in the course of a few days nearly all in the mill were hopefully converted."[1]

EVERYTHING AROUND GOD IS ON FIRE

You may wonder why I am talking specifically about "fire." The answer is, there is one commonality with every supernatural account in history and *it's that of fire*. Men and women who walked with great boldness and power did so because they were baptized with the very presence and power of God's fire.

Our God is a God of fire, in fact, He is an all-consuming fire. You cannot be wholly given to Him and overtaken by Him without eventually coming into contact with this part of who He is. Everything around God is on fire, beginning with His throne.

I watched till thrones were put in place, and the Ancient of Days was seated; His garment was white as snow, and the hair of His head was like wool. His throne was a fiery flame, its wheels a burning fire; a fiery stream issued and came forth from before Him; a thousand thousands ministered to Him; ten thousand times ten thousand stood before Him... (Daniel 7:9-10).

And in the midst of the seven lampstands One like the Son of Man, clothed with a garment down to the feet and girded about the chest with a golden band. His head and hair were white like wool, as white as snow, and His eyes like a flame of fire; His feet were like fine brass, as if refined in a furnace, and His voice as the sound of many waters; He had in His right hand seven stars, out of His mouth went a sharp two-edged sword, and His countenance was like the sun shining in its strength (Revelation 1:13-16).

This is one of my favorite portions of Scripture. We get to see what Jesus looks like today. What I am most fascinated with are His eyes! His *"eyes like a flame of fire"* speak of His burning desire of love, His intensity, and His knowledge that penetrates all things, just as fire penetrates all things, even metal. They speak of His ability to *see* everything, to *feel* love for us, to *impart* love to us, and to *destroy* all that hinders love. God connects His fire to jealous love. He sees the full truth about us, which is both terrifying and wonderful.

Around God's throne are also angels called *seraphim*. The word literally means, "burning ones." In Isaiah 6:1-2 they are described as fiery, six-winged beings that fly around God's throne. When Isaiah saw them he was overcome with the awe-inspiring sight of the six-winged seraphim above the Lord.

The Holy Spirit is also known as "the Spirit of burning." The Holy Spirit manifests around the throne as seven flaming lamps of fire. The number seven speaks of perfect wisdom and completeness.

And from the throne proceeded lightnings, thunderings, and voices. Seven lamps of fire were burning before the throne, which are the seven Spirits of God. (Revelation 4:5).

NOTHING IS DONE WITHOUT FIRE

Nothing is ever done by God, without the fire of God.

Everything around God is on fire. The question is are you? He is the God who answers by fire and He is the

God who came to send fire. Is your furnace filled with the fire of the Holy Spirit? Or is there the strange fire of another god on your altar? Do you have the fire of the Holy Spirit or the strange fire of religion and sophistication? What if today we surrendered to the fire of the Holy Spirit? Jesus is longing to send fire on this city. Only men and women on fire can change neighborhoods, cities, and nations.[2]

THE GOSPEL OF POWER

And my speech and my preaching were not with persuasive words of human wisdom, but in demonstration of the Spirit and of power, that your faith should not be in the wisdom of men but in the power of God (1 Corinthians 2:4-5).

The preaching of the gospel has to be twofold: show and tell. When a man on fire preaches the gospel, he comes with a demonstration of the Spirit's power. This power comes so that people's faith is not established on man's wisdom or on a personality, but on God and God alone.

The gospel is alive and should be preached with power. What kind of power? Healings, signs, wonders, repentance, and salvation accompanied by the fire of God.

The greatest miracle that is a sign and wonder is the turning of a heart to Jesus. Power should be led by an outside representation of who God is. God desires to draw, heal, restore, redeem, forgive, and deliver. Too many people are broken, sick, and in bondage to the devil. If the gospel is freedom—and it is—there is a magnificent power that can set people free of any sickness, disease, or bondage people find themselves in. It's the anointing that breaks the yoke of bondage, not pretty words. We don't need a sales pitch when preaching the gospel;

we need the anointing and power of His Spirit upon our speech that will set people free. We don't need more relevance; we need the fire of God poured out through people who are burning for Him.

God has anointed us to preach the gospel, to proclaim good news to the poor, bind up the brokenhearted, proclaim freedom to captives, and release from darkness those who are prisoners (see Isa. 61:1-3).

If the gospel is not preached with power, then we are not sharing the complete gospel message. I would also say we are not preaching the Jesus of the Bible. If our message is not accompanied by a demonstration of power, the alarming part is that it can be built or established on human wisdom or persuasiveness of speech, and it will not take deep root in the heart and life of the new believer.

Jesus and the apostles showed this by example. The gospel was preached with corresponding power; let's contend for the fullness of this!

> *Jesus went throughout Galilee, teaching in their synagogues, proclaiming the good news of the kingdom, and healing every disease and sickness among the people* (Matthew 4:23 NIV).

> [The apostles] *went out and preached that people should repent. They drove out many demons and anointed many sick people with oil and healed them.* (Mark 6:12-13 NIV).

Jesus sent out the seventy disciples, saying:

> *Heal the sick who are there and tell them, "The kingdom of God has come near you"* (Luke 10:9 NIV).

Reinhard Bonnke, a present-day Christian leader and missionary to Africa—and I would add, "man on fire"— moves in great power, signs, and wonders. Bonnke said,

The Gospel is a hot gospel….The Gospel is, and must be, on fire. To preach the Gospel coolly and casually would be ridiculous.

One day a lady told me that there was a demon sitting on her, although she was a born-again Christian. I said to her, "Flies can only sit on a cold stove, and on a cold stove they can sit very long! Get the fire of the Holy Spirit into your life, that dirty demon will not dare to touch you, lest he burn his filthy fingers."[3]

BAPTISM OF FIRE

John answered, saying to all, "I indeed baptize you with water; but One mightier than I is coming, whose sandal strap I am not worthy to loose. He will baptize you with the Holy Spirit and fire. His winnowing fan is in His hand, and He will thoroughly clean out His threshing floor, and gather the wheat into His barn; but the chaff He will burn with unquenchable fire" (Luke 3:16-17).

John emphasized Jesus as the Baptizer of the Spirit and fire. We've heard accounts of John the Baptist but how many times have we heard a sermon on Jesus the Baptizer? John baptized in water, but Jesus came to baptize with the Holy Spirit and with fire! There were four times that John declared Jesus as the Baptizer (see Matt. 3:11; Mark 1:8; Luke 3:16; John 1:33). All of these, of course, are separate accounts of the same occasion.

When Jesus baptizes with the Spirit, He first baptizes you with power of holiness. He is first Holy. He will drench you in power to be holy. Purity and power are twin results when you're baptized in the Holy Spirit.[4]

What I want us to realize is that it is Jesus Himself who baptizes us with the Holy Spirit and fire. I want us to get away from the idea that it is "something that happens to us" and understand that it is "someone who ministers to us." That someone is Jesus Himself!

PROMISED HOLY SPIRIT

Jesus told His disciples before He ascended that the baptism He promised would take place in just a few days. Jack Hayford illustrates the sequence of things that happened that day beautifully:

When the day came and the power of the Lord fell upon them and filled them, a whole series of things began to happen in their lives:

- As tongues of fire came upon them, they *"began to speak in other tongues as the Spirit enabled them"* (Acts 2:4 NIV).

- A large crowd was attracted and became curious, asking what it was all about (Acts 2:12).

- Peter was gifted to preach the Scriptures with revelatory insight (Acts 2:14,40).

- Multitudes repented and accepted the message of Christ (Acts 2:37,41).

- There was fervent devotion to the Word of God, prayer and to fellowship (Acts 2:42,46).

- Miracles occurred and continued to take place in the lives of the believers. They moved in a spirit of faith that could only have been brought about by the Holy Spirit (Acts 2:43).

- The love of God was manifest in the community of believers as they began caring for each other sacrificially (Acts 2:44-45).[5]

This is not for yesterday or only for the Book of Acts. Jesus is our baptizer and He is ready to baptize us, if we are ready to receive this baptism. This is a baptism of the Holy Spirit and of fire. This can be yours today and fully operational in your life. Every one of those things that happened in the lives of the apostles in the Book of Acts is available to us today, as we receive it from Jesus, our Baptizer.

RECEIVE NOW

If you have not already received the fullness of the Holy Spirit, let me urge you to come to Jesus now. Talk to Him today and ask Him. Here is a suggested prayer that you can use:

Jesus, I come before You. I thank You for Your love and faithfulness to me. Thank You for dying on the cross for my sins and washing me from my sins. I thank You, Jesus, that the vessel of my life is worthy to be filled with the Holy Spirit of God. I want to overflow with Your power and life. I ask you that You would fill me with Your power. I ask You to baptize me with Your Spirit and with fire. I ask You to release Your fire on my life. I receive You today. I receive You fully. Fill my lips, give me boldness, and release Your power on my life today! In Jesus' name. Amen.

Conclusion

OUR RESPONSE

What I am anxious to see in Christian believers
is a beautiful paradox. I want to see in them the
joy of finding God while at the same time they are
blessedly pursuing Him. I want to see in them the
great joy of having God yet always wanting Him.
—A.W. TOZER

IN THIS INCREDIBLE journey of pursuing God there is a great paradox. We get one small taste of Him and it leaves us longing for more. It is completely satisfying, yet it makes us thirsty.

Pursuing God is and has always been a response back to God and His extraordinary love. God Himself first placed this magnificent love within us. We love God because and only because He first loved us (see 1 John 4:19). One touch of this great love on our hearts leaves us undone. He initiates the whole thing. This is what I call the *relentless pursuit*. In this pursuit, there is *seeking* and *finding*. If we seek Him we will find Him, as long as we seek Him with *all* of our hearts. God wants us to draw near to Him and He will draw near to us. The incredible thing is that He beckons us first.

This paradox in the pursuit is a wonderful way to live. A.W. Tozer said, "I want to see in them the great joy of having God yet always wanting Him." God loves our seeking. He loves our reaching and He absolutely loves our wholehearted pursuit after Him in response to His love. Even if what we have to offer God feels small to us, it is great to Him because it is our whole heart.

Pursuing God is a response. It is not forced, it's our response to what we see and taste in Him. As we taste and see that He is good, the love within us grows and matures.

Pursuing God is a focus. Pursuing God is a deliberate, disciplined and sacrificial love offering that lays down all of our heart, mind, soul, and strength. Pursuing God is the first commandment, the pursuit of our first love, placing Him first in our lives!

Can you imagine an earthly relationship when only one person is reaching out for the other, but getting no response back? God has wholeheartedly been pursuing us, but some of us are not awakened to His great love and some have allowed their love to grow cold. Despite it all, He never stops reaching for us. The very thought of this overwhelms me!

SEARCH HIM

It is the glory of God to conceal a matter, but the glory of kings is to search out a matter (Proverbs 25:2).

There is an inheritance for us. We are our Bridegroom God's inheritance. He has hidden His glory for the few who choose to search Him out with full abandonment. It's only the hungry ones who will really search Him out. Those who really want more will never give up. They have a sustained reach. They refuse to be denied.

He desires to be sought after with desperation. He even hides so that we would search for Him. If we seek Him like this, He will surprise us. He will overwhelm us. He is to be discovered little by little.

When one characteristic is revealed, it leaves us awestruck and we keep coming back for more.

It's Him you are hungry for. He created you to thirst after Him, that you would seek Him. Your hunger is the evidence of His desire over you. He is asking you to set your heart toward Him.

He is looking for a people who have their hearts postured toward Him. He wants all of our thoughts and affections to be directed toward Him. Do you know why He wants this kind of response? Because He loves us in the same way. I am overwhelmed with the thought that He loves you and me with all of His heart. That is an incredible reality. God loves us with everything in Him: all of His heart, mind, soul, and strength. All of His love is directed toward us.

In this closing chapter, let me share with you something that I hope will propel and provoke you to reach out for Him like never before. Let's look at the life of John, the disciple whom the Lord loved. As you read this I urge you to make it the dream of your heart.

JOHN THE BELOVED

James...and John...to whom He gave the name..."Sons of Thunder" (Mark 3:17).

The "thunder of John's heart" initially was expressed in his fleshly personality. Our heart naturally thunders with ambition, lust, rejection, anger, bitterness, fear....[1]

John wrote his gospel near the end of his life.

In John 21:20, he wrote his "signature" for his life work. In this verse, he interpreted what it meant to him to live as a "son of Thunder."[2]

This verse tells us how John carried his heart and expressed his highest life goal, his primary dream.

When I started writing this book, I started by refocusing us to the fact that He is our great reward: the One we are looking for. God Himself is our primary goal and primary dream!

> *Peter...saw the disciple whom Jesus loved* [John] *following, who also had leaned on His breast at the supper, and said, "Lord, who is the one who betrays You?"* (John 21:20).

What is astounding to me is that John declared himself to be the one whom Jesus loved. What an amazing revelation he had of Jesus' heart for him. John wanted to be known by his close relationship to Jesus, not by what he accomplished before men. He let us into his view of himself as a lover of Jesus and the confidence that we should have that we are the Lord's favorite!

> John had one of the greatest "resumes" in history being in relationship with Mary (John 19:26-27) and the original apostles, including Paul. John was instrumental in great revivals.... John wrote five books of the [New Testament]. He, was promised to rule on a throne in Israel (Matt 19:28) and saw his name on one of the foundations in the New Jerusalem (Rev. 21:14). Yet John never mentions his own name in the gospel he wrote but refers to himself five times as "the disciple whom the Lord loved" (John 13:23; 19:26; 20:2; 21:7,20).[3]

John leaned on Jesus' heart and set his own heart to love Jesus and be as near to Him as possible. This was John's primary life dream. It was his greatest prayer and desire. John had a masculine personality, but was not at all ashamed to be known as the one who loved Jesus.

> *Because he has set his love upon Me, therefore I will deliver him...* (Psalm 91:14).

John leaned on Jesus' heart at the last supper, "soon after Jesus rebuked him three times for his wrong spirit (Luke 9:46-56; John13:23). John had boldness in Jesus' love without shame...."[4] He did not let the rebuke of Jesus hinder him from drawing close to Him. "John positioned himself to receive the secrets of Jesus' heart."[5] How do we practically receive Jesus' secrets? By sitting at His feet to hear His Word as Mary of Bethany did.[6]

Jesus is our great reward and we can gain insight into what is near and dear to His heart from Scripture, communion, and dreams. One way we do this is "by long hours in prayerful meditation on the Scripture,"[7] and dialoguing with God about the Word. Jesus defined this as good. "No one can choose this for us. We [must] choose to do this over and over."[8]

> *...Mary...sat at Jesus' feet and heard His word. But Martha was distracted with much serving.... And Jesus answered and said to her "...One thing is needed, and Mary has chosen that good part, which will not be taken away from her"* (Luke 10:39-42).

Some search the Word only to prepare a message to speak to others, instead of to encounter God. Some do not even search it at all.

In contrast, Mary of Bethany had no public teaching ministry. She sat at Jesus' feet to understand His heart. Determining what it means to spend long hours with God is different for each person.

God gives His secrets to those who desire them enough to sit before Him. John sat "before God long hours as David did (Ps. 27:4). The Book of Revelation was one of the greatest secrets...given to John."[9] *The secret of the LORD is with those who fear Him...* (Ps. 25:14).

We embrace a right mindset in becoming "sons of thunder in the Spirit" by setting our vision to go deep in God and making Jesus the primary reward and dream of our lives. "We must see ourselves differently and change our confession before God. We are those who are loved by Jesus, who lean on His heart"[10] in our love for Him, and who seek to know His secrets. Whenever we stumble, we repent and confess what God's Word says is true about us. "Even in our weakness, we are the ones that He deeply loves" and delights in (see Ps. 18:19; Isa. 62:4).[11]

I DARE YOU

As I end this book, I leave you with two "dares." I *dare* you to go after God with everything in you. I *dare* you to spend your whole life, affections, and resources on pursuing the heart and face of God. This has been God's heart cry throughout the ages—a people who would desire to know Him in response to His desire for them! To those who dare to draw close to experience intimacy with Him, He shares secrets that no one else will know.

You will be moved to the very core as you encounter the Desire of your life. This is what it's all about. I pray that you have been awakened to God's great pursuit over you and that you sign up to be a wholehearted pursuer of His great love.

We are part of the greatest love story ever told—and we are in *relentless pursuit* for all eternity.

ENDNOTES

CHAPTER 1: THE INVITATION

1. Bill Johnson, *Face to Face with God* (Lake Mary, FL: Charisma House, 2007), 3.

CHAPTER 2: RELENTLESS PURSUIT

1. Mike Bickle, "Studies in the Bride of Christ, Part 10: The Bridegroom God and His Bride—Old Testament Overview," December 10, 2010, audio and transcript, http://mikebickle.org/resources/resource/2986?return_url=http%3A%2F%2Fmikebickle.org%2Fresources%2Fseries%2Fthe-bride-of-christ-2010 (accessed February 16, 2013).

CHAPTER 3: IGNITING A HEART

1. Mike Bickle, "The First Commandment, Session 1: Loving God: The First and Great Commandment," August 22, 2008, transcript, 16, http://www.mikebickle.org.edgesuite.net/MikeBickleVOD/2008/20080822-T-Loving_God_The_First_and_Great_Commandment_TFC01.pdf (accessed February 16, 2013).

2. Mike Bickle, *The Beatitudes; The Only Way to Happiness and Greatness,* November 26, 2006, International House of Prayer, Kansas City, www.mikebickle.org

CHAPTER 4: KNOWING GOD

1. A.W. Tozer, *The Pursuit of God,* (Camp Hill, PA: Wing Spread Publishers, 1982, 1993), 33.

2. Stephen Arterburn and Debra Cherry, *Feeding Your Appetites: Take Control of What's Controlling You!* (Nashville, Tennessee: Thomas Nelson, 2004), 150-151.

CHAPTER 5: WALKING IT OUT

1. Hudson Taylor, "The Source of Power," from *Report of the Ecumenical Conference on Foreign Missions, Vol. I* (New York: American Tract Society, 1900), 88.

2. Mike Bickle, *Forerunner School of Ministry* "Seven Commitments of a Forerunner," August 7, 2009, transcript, Kansas City, Missouri, www.mikebickle.org.

3. Mike Bickle, *Prayers to Strengthen Your Inner Man,* (Kansas City, MO: Forerunner Publishing, 2009), 4.

4. Mike Bickle, "How To Develop a Strong Prayer Life," notes, http://www.mikebickle.org.edgesuite.net/MikeBickleVOD/2010/20101015_How_to_Develop_A_Strong_Prayer_Life_IPP01.pdf, 2.

CHAPTER 6: LIFE WITH VISION

1. Greta Van Susteren, Interview, *Fox News Channel,* December 21, 2010.

2. Christian Classics Ethereal Library, Jonathan Edwards, www.ccel.org.

3. Steven J. Lawson, *The Unwavering Resolve of Jonathan Edwards* (Lake Mary, FL: Reformation Trust, 2008), 95.

4. Ibid., 107.

5. Ibid., 158.

6. Mike Bickle with Brian Kim, *7 Commitments of a Forerunner* (Kansas City, MO: Forerunner Publishing, 2009), 108.

7. Craig Cook, "Our Plumb Line to the Great Commandment," December 2, 2012, www.hopevansville.org (accessed February 21, 2013).

8. Zig Ziglar, "Goal Setting," www.goals2go.com.

9. List adapted from George T. Doran, "Creating S.M.A.R.T. Goals," Top Achievement, http://topachievement.com/smart .html (accessed February 21, 2013).

10. "Prayer Quotes," Prayer for All People, http://prayerforallpeople .com/pquotes.shtml (accessed February 21, 2013).

CHAPTER 7: KEYS TO INTIMACY

1. John Bevere, *Drawing Near: A Life of Intimacy with God* (Nashville, TN: Thomas Nelson Inc., 2004), 126.

2. John G. Lake, *His Life, His Sermons, His Boldness of Faith* (Fort Worth, Texas: Kenneth Copeland Publications, 1994), 397.

3. Bill Johnson, *Face to Face with God*, (Lake Mary, FL: Charisma House, 2007), 21.

CHAPTER 8: PURSUIT OF HOLINESS

1. Francis Frangipane, *Holiness, Truth, and the Presence of God* (Lake Mary, Florida: Charisma House, 2011), E-book, 1.

2. Ibid., 2.

3. Ibid., 14.

4. Ibid., *vii*.

5. Mike Bickle, Cultivating the Oil of Intimacy, April 10, 2010, International House of Prayer Kansas City, www.mikebickle. org

6. Francis Frangipane, *Holiness, Truth, and the Presence of God*, 2.

7. Mike Bickle, "Living Holy: Living Fascinated in the Pleasure of Loving God," transcript, August, 14, 2009, www.mikebickle. org

8. Ibid., 1.

9. Francis Frangipane, *Holiness, Truth, and the Presence of God*, 59.

10. Ibid., 63.

11. Mike Bickle, "Purity Covenant: 7 Practical Commitments," March 30, 2008, , 3 (accessed February 22, 2013).

12. Jonathan Welton, *Eyes of Honor: Training for Purity and Righteousness*, (Shippensburg, PA: Destiny Image Publishers, Inc., 2012), 155.

13. Mike Bickle, "Fellowshipping with The Holy Spirit," March 8, 2007, , 1 (accessed February 22, 2013).

14. Ibid.

15. Ibid.

16. Ibid., 3.

17. Ibid.

18. Ibid., 4.

CHAPTER 9: POWER BEHIND THE GREATS

1. Billy Graham, *The Journey* (Nashville, Tennessee: W Publishing Group, A Division of Thomas Nelson, Inc., 2006), 101-103.

2. God's Generals Christian History, "Evan Roberts," http://www .godsgenerals.com/person_e_roberts.htm (accessed February 21, 2013).

3. John Emery, *The Works of Reverand John Wesley*, A.M. Volume 1, (published by J. Emory and B. Waugh, 1831), 261.

4. Elizabeth George, *A Women's Guide to Making Right Choices* (Harvest House Publishing, 2012), 107.

5. Eliza Clark, *Susanna Wesley* (London: W.H. Allen & Co, 1886), 205.

6. Thomas Jackson, *The Life of the Rev. Charles Wesley* (MA, G. Lane & P. P. Sandford for the Methodist Episcopal Church, 1842), 222.

7. God's Generals Christian History, "John G. Lake," http://www .godsgenerals.com/person_j_lake.htm (accessed February 21, 2013).

8. "History of John G. Lake," Healing Rooms Ministries, http:// healingrooms.com/index.php?page_id=422 (accessed February 21, 2013).

9. Ibid.

10. Ibid.

11. Roberts Liardon, *God's Generals* (Whitaker House Publishing, 1996), 189.

12. Jonathan Edwards, Henry Rogers, Gereno Edwards Dwight, Edwards Hickman, *The Works of Jonathan Edwards, A.M.,* Volume II, (London: Ball, Arnold, and Co., 1840), 72.

13. God's Generals Christian History, "Jonathan Edwards," http:// www.godsgenerals.com/person_jonathan-edwards.htm (accessed February 21, 2013).

14. http://www.amazon.com/wiki/Jonathan_Edwards_(theologian)/ ref=ntt_at_bio_wiki.

15. *Wikipedia,* "First Great Awakening," (accessed February 23, 2013).

16. Jonathan Edwards, *The Life and Diary of David Brainerd* (Grand Rapids: Baker Books, 1989), 76.

17. God's Faithbook, "Wednesday, May 23 - Session 12, Part IX - Intercessor: David Brainerd," http://www.godsfaithbook.com/index.php?option=com_community&view=groups&task=view discussion&groupid=176&topicid=3560&Itemid=101 (accessed February 23, 2013).

18. Ibid.

19. E.M. Bounds, *The Complete Works of E.M. Bounds on Prayer* (Grand Rapids, MI: Baker Books, 1990), 432.

20. Jonathan Edwards, *The Life and Diary of David Brainerd* (Grand Rapids: Baker Books, 1989), 76.

21. Ibid., 79.

22. Ibid., 80.

23. Ibid., 82.

24. Ibid., 83.

25. Ibid., 96.

26. Ibid., 215.

27. Ibid., 216-217.

28. Jonathan Edwards, et al, *The Works of Jonathan Edwards, A.M., Volume II, 393.*

CHAPTER 10: FOLLOWING OUR FATHERS

1. John Piper, *Hunger For God* (Wheaton, Illinois: Crossway Publisher, 1997), 13.

2. Mike Bickle, "Being Taught to Pray by Jesus," notes, October 14, 2012, http://www.mikebickle.org.edgesuite.net/MikeBickleVOD/2012/20121014_Being_Taught_to_Pray_by_Jesus.pdf (accessed February 23, 2013), 1.

3. Ibid.

4. Ibid.

5. Ibid., 2.

6. Ibid.

7. Ibid., 3.

8. Ibid.

9. Ibid.

10. Ibid.

11. Ibid.

12. Ibid.

13. Ibid.

14. Ibid., 4.

15. Ibid.

16. Ibid.

17. Ibid.

18. Ibid.

CHAPTER 12: FASTED LIFESTYLE

1. Mike Bickle and Dana Candler, *The Rewards of Fasting* (Kansas City, MO: Forerunner Books, 2005), 89-90.

2. Ibid., 90.

3. Mike Bickle, *7 Commitments of a Forerunner* (Kansas City, MO: Forerunner Books, 2009), 57-58. Breaks were inserted in text for easy reference.

4. Ibid., 58.

5. Ibid.

CHAPTER 13: MORAVIAN PASSION

1. http://www.historymakers.info/inspirational-christians/ count-zinzendorf.html

2. Rick Joyner, *Three Witnesses: John Huss, Jon Amos Comenius, and Count Nikolaus von Zinzendorf* (Fort Hills, South Carolina: Morningstar Publications, Inc., 2010), 1997, E-Book Edition, 275.

3. Ibid., 305.

4. Ibid., 571.

5. Ibid., 684.

6. Ibid., 699.

7. Ibid., 811.

8. Ibid., 828.

9. Ibid., 944.

10. Stephen Venable, *Foundations of Night and Day Worship,* (Session 05, International House of Prayer University 2010), 11.

11. Ibid., 7.

12. Ibid., 8.

13. Ibid., 13.

14. "Foundations of Night and Day Worship," (Session 6, International House of Prayer University 2010), 06, 1.

15. Ibid., 3.

16. Ibid., 10.

17. Ibid., 10.

CHAPTER 14: BURN FOR HIM

1. Charles G. Finney, *Memoirs of Charles G. Finney,* (New York: A.S. Barnes and Company, 1896), 183-184.

2. Allen Hood, *The Baptism and Ministry of Fire,* (International House of Prayer, Kansas City, Missouri), 12.

3. Reinhard Bonnke, *Evangelism by Fire,* (Lake Mary, Florida: Charisma House), 26-27.

4. David Pawson, *Jesus Baptizes in One Holy Spirit*, (Terra Nova Publications International, 2010), Avon, Wiltshire, E-Book, 829.

5. Jack Hayford, *Explaining Baptism with the Holy Spirit*, (Sovereign World LTD), E-Books, Ellel, Lancaster, UK, 2012 Edition, Loc.176.

CONCLUSION: OUR RESPONSE

1. Mike Bickle, *The Forerunner School of Ministry*, "John the Apostle: His Three-fold Spiritual Identity," June 27, 2008, 1 (accessed March 1, 2013).

2. Ibid., 2.

3. Ibid.

4. Ibid., 3.

5. Ibid.

6. Ibid.

7. Ibid.

8. Ibid.

9. Ibid., 4.

10. Ibid., 5.

11. Ibid.

ABOUT
ANTONIO BALDOVINOS

Marked by boldness and passion, Antonio Baldovinos has an uncompromising message of calling the Church to a whole-hearted pursuit after God. Since 2000 Antonio has traveled to many nations seeing tens of thousands respond to the gospel. In 2008 God expanded his vision to call people to a lifestyle of prayer and intimacy with God. It is this passion that brought him and his wife to establish the Global Prayer House Missions Base, which includes the Pursuit Conference, the Pursuit Internship, and the Pursuit Worship, all flowing out of the place of prayer and worship. Antonio and his beautiful wife, Christelle, live in Alberta, Canada and love raising their five children: Michael, Gabriel, Elijah, Isabella, and Justice.

CONTACT:

Website: www.antoniobaldovinos.org
Email: info@antoniobaldovinos.org
Twitter: @Antoniobaldov

MORE ABOUT ANTONIO'S MINISTRY

Global Prayer House: www.globalprayerhouse.com
Pursuit Conferences: www.pursuitmovement.com
Pursuit Internship: www.pursuitinternship.com